LOTUS® SPREADSHEET
TO ACCOMPANY GUILTIN

MARKETING MANAGEMENT
STRATEGIES AND PROGRAMS
FOURTH EDITION

C. ANTHONY DI BENEDETTO
Temple University

McGRAW-HILL, INC.
New York   St. Louis   San Francisco   Auckland   Bogotá   Caracas
Hamburg   Lisbon   London   Madrid   Mexico   Milan   Montreal   New Delhi
Paris   San Juan   São Paulo   Singapore   Sydney   Tokyo   Toronto

LOTUS® SPREADSHEET PROBLEMS
TO ACCOMPANY GUILTINAN / PAUL
MARKETING MANAGEMENT: STRATEGIES AND PROGRAMS
FOURTH EDITION

Copyright © 1991 by McGraw-Hill, Inc. All rights reserved. Printed in the United States of America. Except as permitted under the United States Copyright Act of 1976, no part of this publication may be reproduced or distributed in any form or by any means, or stored in a data base or retrieval system, without the prior written permission of the publisher.

1 2 3 4 5 6 7 8 9 0   MAL MAL   9 0 9 8 7 6 5 4 3 2 1

P/N 837802-8

The editors were Bonnie Binkert and Mimi Melek;
the production supervisor was Anthony DiBartolomeo.
Malloy Lithographing, Inc. was printer and binder.

IBM is a registered trademark of International Business Machines Corporation.
Lotus 1-2-3 is a registered trademark of Lotus Development Corporation.

TABLE OF CONTENTS

	Page
NOTES TO THE STUDENT	v
PART 1: PRACTICE PROBLEMS	1
1.1 B & G Electronics (BANDG)	2
1.2 Trend Analysis Using Regression (TREND)	7
PART 2: FORECASTING	11
2.1 Warrior Systems (WARRIOR)	12
2.2 Bass Model Exercise (BASS)	14
2.3 The Adventure Park, Inc. (ADVENTUR)	16
2.4 Development of a Forecasting Model (CURVES)	18
PART 3: PROFITABILITY AND PRODUCTIVITY ANALYSIS	21
3.1 Midwest Leather Products (MIDWEST)	22
3.2 E-Z Fresh Rug Cleaner (EZFRESH)	26
3.3 Gateway Company (GATEWAY)	28
3.4 Imperial Camera Shop (IMPERIAL)	29
3.5 Top System Carpet Cleaning (TOPSYS)	31
3.6 Greenspray, Inc. (GSPRAY)	34
PART 4: PRODUCT PROGRAMS	39
4.1 Lucas Company (LUCAS)	40
4.2 Mitchell Stationery Company (MITCHELL)	42
4.3 Assessor Exercise (ASSESSOR)	44
4.4 Product Positioning Using Perceptor (PERCEPT)	47
4.5 Conquer Brand Analgesic (CONQUER)	50
PART 5: PRICING PROGRAMS	53
5.1 Corbett Company (CORBETT)	54
5.2 Cost-Plus Pricing Exercise (COSTPLUS)	56
5.3 National Electric (NATIONAL)	58
5.4 Eastside Construction Co. (EASTSIDE)	60
5.5 Business Applications, Inc. (BUSINESS)	62
PART 6: ADVERTISING PROGRAMS	65
6.1 General Brands (GENERAL)	66
6.2 Sunscreen, Inc. (SUNSCR)	69
6.3 Vidale-Wolfe Model Exercise (VIDALE)	71
6.4 Whittaker Products, Inc. (WHITT)	73
6.5 Media Planning Exercise (MEDIAE)	75

PART 7: SALES PROMOTION PROGRAMS   79
    7.1 Gasoline Promotion Model (GASOLINE)   80
    7.2 Harris Company (HARRIS)   83
    7.3 Treasure Isle Seafood Company (TREASURE)   85
    7.4 Chef Alphonse (ALPHONSE)   88
    7.5 Burger Master (BURGER)   91

PART 8: SALES AND DISTRIBUTION PROGRAMS   95
    8.1 Handel, Inc. (HANDEL)   96
    8.2 Colbert Company (COLBERT)   98
    8.3 Litebar, Inc. (LITEBAR)   100
    8.4 Easterly Floor Coverings (EASTERLY)   102
    8.5 Sales Force Call Planning Exercise (SFCALL)   104

PART 9: THE MARKETING PLAN   107
    9.1 Nor-East Dairies (NOREAST)   108
    9.2 Goodwell Company (GOODWELL)   111
    9.3 Elliott Corporation (ELLIOTT)   113
    9.4 Harpswell, Inc. (HARPSWEL)   116
    9.5 Worldwide Food Products, Inc. (WORLD)   119

REFERENCES   122

NOTES TO THE STUDENT

This set of problems has been designed to give you practice making realistic marketing decisions with the use of business spreadsheetson the personal computer. If you are not familiar with LOTUS 123 or similar spreadsheet packages, fear not! You do not need to do any LOTUS programming in doing these problems. The programming has already been done, and you will find practice problems and other guidance to help you along the way. In fact, this is an excellent opportunity for you to familiarize yourself with business spreadsheets.

In today's business environment, much information is available to the business manager, and quantitative skills are a must. Managers in all areas of marketing analyze numbers: they develop sales quotas, media schedules, five-year business plans, industry forecasts, and program effectiveness measures; and they conduct many other kinds of analyses. You will probably be at a disadvantage when you enter the job market and later in your career if you do not have basic familiarity with the computer and with interpreting the results it gives you.

You should set goals for yourself in doing these problems. By the time the course is over, you should feel as _comfortable_ using the personal computer for numerical analysis as you do using your pocket calculator. Also, you should view spreadsheet analysis as a _means to an end_: making better business decisions. If you feel unsure of your abilities on the computer, try the two simple practice problems. They come with plenty of instructions and serve as handy references for later on. The practice problems should help convince you that the computer is not something to fear.

Keep these goals in mind as you do the problems you are assigned. As you are working out problems, remember that the objective is not to number crunch dozens of spreadsheets and hand them in to the instructor. In each problem, you have a marketing decision to make: set a sales goal for a product that enables you to make a profit, determine whether a proposed coupon promotion should be executed, plan a product repositioning, and so on. The computer analysis you carry out _helps you to make that decision_; it is the means to an end. In the long run, the interpretations and recommendations you make, based on your computer analysis, are what count.

If you approach these problems as "_marketing decision-making_ problems in which I happen to use a personal computer to assist in the numerical analysis," and not "_computer_ problems," they will be more valuable to you.

The problems are geared to the numerical problems found in the fourth edition of Guiltinan and Paul's <u>Marketing Management: Strategies and Programs</u> textbook. Included are problems on forecasting, contribution analysis, each of the marketing programs (product, pricing, advertising, sales promotion, selling and distribution), and business planning. Some of the problems are very similar to those appearing in the textbook, while others are applications or extensions of textbook material. Each category progresses from rather simple exercises to more advanced problems.

Although the practice problems will give you much more detailed help, here are a few "ground rules" that will take you through most of the problems:

1. When you make changes in a spreadsheet, make sure you change ONLY those numbers indicated by arrows (<<). You will be able to answer all of the required questions by making changes to these indicated numbers. Changing other numbers on a spreadsheet might cause you to lose an important equation and thus make the rest of your analysis incorrect.

2. Each problem is equipped with macro commands that allow you to do various things: print a spreadsheet, draw a graph, change spreadsheet values, and so on. These will simplify your analysis. Note that if you do not have a graphics monitor, you will not be able to display the graphs you draw on your screen. You will still be able to save your graph, however, and print it later on a graphics printer.

3. A few of the problems require you to do a regression analysis. You will need LOTUS Release 2.0 or higher to do these problems, as Release 1 does not support data regression.

<u>Important Note</u>

Before getting started, MAKE A COPY of the Problem Disk you received on a new disk, and use your copy for carrying out your analyses. The disk you received is a READ ONLY DISK, so you will not be able to save any spreadsheets or PrintGraph files on it. Better still, find out from your instructor which files you will be needing for this course, and COPY ONLY THOSE ON YOUR NEW DISK. This is a good idea because the Problem Disk is almost full, and you will soon run out of room on it for storing spreadsheets and PrintGraph files. Remember, by working on your copy only, you always have the original Problem Disk for backup in case you accidentally erase some of your files.

PART 1: PRACTICE PROBLEMS

   1.1 B & G Electronics (BANDG)
1.2 Trend Analysis Using Regression (TREND)

File Name: BANDG

1.1 B & G ELECTRONICS

(This problem involves a simple contribution analysis. It comes with full instructions for LOTUS: how to load the spreadsheet, make changes, print, save your work, and exit. Some helpful hints on problem solution are also provided. This problem can be used as a step-by-step guide if you have little or no experience with spreadsheet analysis.)

B & G manufactures a video game popular with the teenage market. The product sells to retailers for $20 per unit. Retailers charge $45 for the game, and manufacturer's variable production costs are $12. Direct fixed costs for marketing are $1.4 million, and industry sales are forecasted for the coming year at 3 million units, reflecting no change from the current year. The company now holds a 10% market share. (See Exhibit 1 for Contribution Margin Statement.)

1. Suppose manufacturer's selling price were to decrease from $20 to $18. How would B & G's sales revenue and contribution to indirect costs and profit (C.I.C.P.) change? What if manufacturer's selling price were $16?

2. Set manufacturer's selling price back to $20. If variable costs of production were to increase to $13, how would that affect B & G's contribution?

3. Set variable costs of production back to $12. B & G is considering a $200,000 increase in the advertising budget for next year. What level of market share at retail would be required to maintain the product's current total contribution to indirect costs and profit?

4. Suppose top management would like this product's contribution to indirect costs and profit to increase by $100,000 (in addition to the advertising increase already mentioned). What would be the required market share at retail to meet this objective?

Exhibit 1. B & G Electronics Contribution Analysis

Retail selling price:	$45
Manuf. selling price:	$20<<
Variable costs of prodn.:	$12<<
Direct fixed costs:	$1,400,000<<
Ind. sales forecast:	3000000
Projected market share:	10%<<

Contribution Margin Statement

Retail sales dollars	$13,500,000
- Retail margin	$7,500,000
Manuf. sales dollars	$6,000,000
- Manuf. variable costs	$3,600,000
Variable contribution	$2,400,000
- Fixed costs	$1,400,000
Contrib. to indirect costs and profit	$1,000,000

DOING THE B & G CASE ON THE COMPUTER

TO START

If you have a two-floppy-drive system, put the LOTUS System Disk in Drive A and your Problem Disk in Drive B. Type **123** and hit **Return**, and wait for the blank spreadsheet to appear on the screen.

If you have a hard disk with LOTUS installed, put your Problem Disk in Drive A. Select the directory containing LOTUS on the hard disk. Type **123**, hit **Return**, and wait for the blank spreadsheet to appear on the screen.

TO SELECT A DIRECTORY

You have to tell the computer which disk to read files from. To do this, type **/FD** ("Slash" File Directory). The computer will ask you to name the current directory. Type the name of the drive with your Problem Disk followed by a colon (type either **A:** or **B:**). Hit **Return** key.

TO LOAD THE B & G FILE

To load any file, type **/FR** ("Slash" File Retrieve). When the computer asks for the file name, either type **BANDG** or use the **Arrow** keys to move the cursor over the name "BANDG.WKS". Hit **Return**. (See what happens if you hit the **Tab** key instead of an **Arrow** key. This might be something to keep in mind for later.)

TO CHANGE VALUES ON SPREADSHEET

To make any changes, move the cursor to the desired cell using the **Arrow** keys. To change a value, type the new value you want and hit **Return**. Your new value should appear in the spreadsheet where the cursor is. Try Questions 1 and 2 for practice.

Notice the upper left corner of the screen. It displays the Cell Contents, that is, what each cell of the spreadsheet actually contains. When the cursor was on the manufacturer's selling price of $20, the upper left corner indicated "20" (the computer automatically added the dollar sign). This shows that the cell contains a value, namely 20. IT IS SAFE TO REPLACE VALUES.

Not all cells contain values. Move the cursor down to the figure for retail sales dollars ($13,500,000). Although the cell <u>displays</u> a number, the upper left corner reveals the Cell Contents to be an equation. IF YOU ENTER A NUMBER HERE, YOU WILL WRITE OVER THE EQUATION AND IT WILL BE LOST. Any further analysis you do will be wrong. A good practice is to check the Cell Contents before making any changes to the spreadsheet.

If you accidentally write over an equation or make some other unwanted change to the spreadsheet, you can always get back to the original spreadsheet by reloading (start over at **/FR**), as long as you did not save your changes.

To be safe, make changes only to cells indicated by arrows (<<) as shown in the spreadsheet on the first page of this problem.

Questions 3 and 4 are a little more complex because you have to use an indirect approach to solve them. In Question 3, you are considering increasing advertising (a direct fixed cost) by $200,000, and you want to know what your market share has to be in order to maintain Contribution to Indirect Costs and Profit (C.I.C.P.) at the current level of $1,000,000. Increase the direct fixed costs figure by the desired amount and notice that C.I.C.P. decreases. Obviously, 10% market share is not enough. To solve this problem, move the cursor to the market share location (currently 10%); try 11%, 12%, 13% and so on; and observe how C.I.C.P. changes. Keep going until you find you have gone too far (C.I.C.P. is greater than $1,000,000) then work backwards and zero in on the required market share. Question 4 is worked the same way.

Note that when you want to enter a percentage (such as a market share), you must use a decimal point. For 10%, enter **.10** or **.1**. For 8%, enter **.08**. The computer automatically converts to percentages.

TO PRINT OUT YOUR RESULTS

You would like to print out the entire screen. The range you want to print out is A1..E20. A1 is the upper left corner of the range, and E20 is the lower right corner. (In LOTUS, you define a range with two periods as shown.) To do this, type **/PPR**. The computer will ask for a Print Range; type **A1..E20** and hit **Return**. Type **AG** (to align the top of your spreadsheet to the beginning of the next page and to go). Your spreadsheet will be printed out. To leave the Print function, type **Q** (Quit).

Note: All problems have a Print macro command, which will execute these steps automatically. Most spreadsheets you will need to print out can be obtained through macros. If you ever need to print out a spreadsheet not available using a macro command, you can follow the steps just described. (See the discussion of macro commands below.)

TO SAVE AND EXIT LOTUS

To save a spreadsheet, type **/FS**. The computer will ask for a name for this file. Simply type the name you want and hit **Return**. Choose a name that is different from the original name, because you may want to recall the original file sometime later. If you choose the original name, the file you are saving will write over the original file, and you will lose it.

To erase a spreadsheet, type **/WEY** (Worksheet Erase Yes). This is handy if you have made a mistake and wish to start over. The spreadsheet should now be blank, and you can call up another.

If you wish to leave LOTUS temporarily but plan to come back to it, type **/S** (System). This will return you to DOS, and you can get back to LOTUS again quickly by typing **Exit**.

To quit the LOTUS session, type **/QY**.

USING MACRO COMMANDS

Each problem has at least one macro command to help you. The B & G problem has the following one:

(Alt)P: To print screen.

This message tells you that if you type **P** while holding down the **Alt** key, the spreadsheet will be printed out automatically. Once you have your printout, you will have to type **Q** to get out of the Print function.

Later problems will have macros to make changes in the spreadsheet, do a regression analysis, save a PrintGraph file, or do other things. You will always be told what macros are available to you and what they do. You can always do these steps "manually" if you prefer not to use the macro commands, although it is recommended that you use the PrintGraph and regression macros when they are available.

File Name: TREND

1.2 TREND ANALYSIS USING REGRESSION

(This problem shows you how to run a trend analysis and also introduces you to some of the problems encountered in using trend analysis forecast sales for a product class. To do this problem, you do not need any prior knowledge of how to run a regression on LOTUS, as the spreadsheet has complete instructions. If you are unfamiliar with LOTUS, though, you would be better off to read the section on running regressions before doing this problem.)

On the accompanying spreadsheet (Exhibit 1), you will find one year's worth, by months, of total industry sales data for a small, frequently purchased consumer good.

1. Do a trend forecast for sales over the next three months using regression.

2. Plot actual (historical) sales figures using PrintGraph, and assess whether the forecast obtained from trend analysis is useful for this problem.

3. What are the possible consequences of overestimating or underestimating future sales?

Exhibit 1. Monthly Sales Data for Industry

Month	Period	19X1
January	1	245
February	2	279
March	3	299
April	4	301
May	5	309
June	6	312
July	7	308
August	8	324
September	9	356
October	10	358
November	11	398
December	12	399
Yearly total		3888

MACRO COMMANDS PROVIDED:
(Alt)P: To print main screen.
(Alt)G: To save PrintGraph file (plot of sales vs. time period).

DOING THE TREND CASE ON THE COMPUTER

TO START

Load the file (see instructions for the B & G problem).

TO DO A REGRESSION

Type **/DR** ("Slash" Data Regression).

You will need to specify the X and Y ranges. In this problem, the X (independent) variable is TIME PERIOD and the Y (dependent) variable is SALES.

Select the "X-Range" using the **Arrow** keys. When cursor is on "X-Range", hit **Return**. The computer will ask for the X variable range. Type **B5..B16** because, as you can see from the spreadsheet, this is where your desired X range (time period) is. Then hit **Return**.

Select "Y-Range", again using the **Arrow** keys, and hit **Return**. When prompted, enter **C5..C16**, because this is where the sales figures are, and hit **Return**.

Now you have to tell the computer where you want your results to be written. Your spreadsheet has a large blank area on the right side of the screen, and it makes sense to have your results printed there. Move the cursor to "Output-Range" and hit **Return**. When asked to enter an output range, type **E5..H13** and hit **Return**.

To do the regression, type **G** for "Go".

INTERPRETING YOUR RESULTS

You will get the following output:

Constant
Standard Error of Y Estimate
R squared
No. of observations
Degrees of Freedom
X Coefficient
Standard Error of X Coefficient

The regression equation you obtain is $Y = AX + B$, where A is the X Coefficient and B is the Constant above. This equation corresponds to a line with Slope A and Y-Intercept B, as shown in Exhibit 2.

The R-squared value is a measure of how much variance in the Y term is explained by the X variable. You may recall another name for

R-squared from your statistics course: the coefficient of determination. You can think of R squared as a measure of "fit"; the higher R-squared is, the better the regression equation "fits" the data points. R-squared is a number between zero and one, so an R-squared value close to one (0.85 or 0.9) is an indication of good fit.

This R-squared value is not adjusted for degrees of freedom, so it is possible that, if your degrees of freedom are very low, R-squared may be misleading. This is a topic you can review in your statistics book or at the library. The standard errors are indications of the significance of the relationship between X and Y. If the standard error of the X Coefficient is low compared to the X Coefficient, it indicates that X (time period in this example) is a significant variable.

Exhibit 2. Regression Line with Slope and Y-Intercept Shown

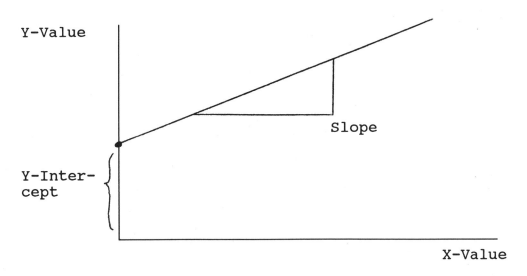

TO CONTINUE WITH PROBLEM

If you have a large LOTUS spreadsheet (as you have with this problem), you will need to page up, down, left or right to get to different portions of the spreadsheet.

Paging up or down is easy; hit the **PgUp** or **PgDn** key. In this problem you must page down to continue.

To page left or right: While keeping the **Ctrl** key down, hit the left or right **Arrow** key. On your spreadsheet, this move is denoted as "**(Ctrl)(Left)**" or "**(Ctrl)(Right)**". Page up, down, left and right to see what you find.

In these problems, you will always get a message on your screen to advise you when there is more of a spreadsheet to see. Incidentally, this problem and some others come with extra information or explanations provided right in the spreadsheet for easy access. If such information is provided, you will be advised with a message like "For more information: (Ctrl)(Right)".

TO PRINT A GRAPH

In Question 2, you must print a graph of sales against time period. To print a graph in LOTUS, you need to save a PrintGraph file. All problems that require you to do any graphing or plotting have a macro command--usually, but not always, (Alt)G--that prepares the file for you automatically. (Try **(Alt)G** now to see what happens.)

After the macro is executed, you can do one of two things:

1. <u>Save</u> the PrintGraph file just specified. To do this, type **S** for save; then, when prompted, type in a name for your file. If you type, say, **JIMMY**, then the computer saves a file called JIMMY.PIC for you. After you are finished with spreadsheet analysis, you can get into PrintGraph (see instructions below) and select the file JIMMY to plot.

2. If you have a graphics monitor, you can first type **V** to see what the PrintGraph file will look like when printed. (If you do not have a graphics monitor, you will get a warning beep.) Once you have viewed the graph, hit any key to return to the spreadsheet; then type **S** to save the file.

After saving the PrintGraph file, you will need to type **Q** to get out of the Graph function.

The steps required to create a PrintGraph file manually are included in the spreadsheet for your information.

GETTING INTO PRINTGRAPH

Once you have exited the spreadsheet (with **/QY**), type **LOTUS**. You should get an introductory menu for LOTUS, which allows you to select 1-2-3, PrintGraph, or several other possibilities. Move the cursor using the **Arrow** keys to "PrintGraph" and hit **Return**.

Once you are in PrintGraph, move the cursor to "Image-Select" and hit **Return**. All the PrintGraph files on your diskette (including "JIMMY" from above) will appear on the screen. Move the cursor with the **Arrow** keys to the desired file; then hit **Return**. Then type **A** to align with the top of the next page, and **G** to go.

If you have problems, you may need to change some of the settings. Consult a LOTUS manual (or, if you are at school or work, a supervisor) for assistance.

When you are through with PrintGraph, select **EY** (Exit Yes).

PART 2: FORECASTING

2.1 Warrior Systems (WARRIOR)
2.2 Bass Model Exercise (BASS)
2.3 The Adventure Park, Inc. (ADVENTUR)
2.4 Development of a Forecasting Model (CURVES)

File Name: WARRIOR (Requires LOTUS Release 2.0 or higher)

2.1 WARRIOR SYSTEMS

Warrior Systems is a large regional distributor of heat pumps, air conditioning units, and furnaces. At the end of the company's 1985 fiscal year, the sales manager was trying to develop marketing plans for the company's major lines. In particular, he was concerned about whether to expand the fleet of trucks used by service personnel responsible for installing equipment and whether to increase inventory levels and the order department staff so that the company could react quickly to inquiries from contractors or individual customers. The first step in the planning process, he decided, would be to develop a sales forecast for heat pumps for the next three quarters based on the historical sales data given in Exhibit 1.

1. Develop a time-series forecast for the next three quarters based on trend-line analysis (i.e., no seasonal effects). What are your projected levels for the next three quarters? Plot a graph showing the historical sales figures and the projections you obtained.

2. Determine the seasonal indices and a revised time-series forecast with seasonal effects. What are your revised projected levels for the next three quarters? Plot a graph showing the historical sales figures and the revised projections.

3. Which of these forecasts would you trust more? Why? Use both your regression analyses and your graphs to answer this question.

4. Would you trust longer-term forecasts made using this method? Why or why not? If not, how could you improve the forecasts?

Exhibit 1. Warrior Systems Sales History

Quarter	Period	Sales
1982-3	1	872
1982-4	2	1029
1983-1	3	1019
1983-2	4	1002
1983-3	5	1024
1983-4	6	1197
1984-1	7	1088
1984-2	8	1092
1984-3	9	1102
1984-4	10	1231
1985-1	11	1244
1985-2	12	1236

MACRO COMMANDS PROVIDED:
(Alt)G and (Alt)H: To save PrintGraph files (nonadjusted and
    seasonally-adjusted sales against quarter).
(Alt)P and (Alt)Q: To print results for nonadjusted and
    seasonally-adjusted regressions.

Note: This problem is based on the Warrior Systems (A) case in Guiltinan and Paul's second edition manual.

File Name: BASS

2.2 BASS MODEL EXERCISE

You are product manager for a brand of a durable good (such as televisions, air-conditioning units, stereos), and you would like to determine future profitability for your brand. One extremely useful number to forecast is product class sales (sales of all televisions including your brand). Suppose you knew that product class sales had been growing rather slowly in recent years. If you forecasted that the product was reaching maturity, and that sales would remain constant over the next five years, you know that you would have to increase your share of the market in order to increase sales (say, from 10% to 12%). If product class sales were going to increase every year for the next few years, your sales would increase even if your share of the market remained constant (say, 10%), since every year you would be getting 10% of a bigger "pie." If you knew your brand's sales and could estimate your future costs, you could assess future profitability. So, the starting point to developing a pro-forma profit statement is determining product class sales. Ideally, you would like to be able to forecast product class sales using data that are relatively easy to obtain.

Professor Frank Bass developed a very useful sales growth model (see Bass 1969) that predicts future product class sales for durable goods using easily obtained data: historical product sales. As Exhibit 1 shows, the model has done a very good job in the past predicting how long it took for product class sales to peak, and what sales levels were in the peak year.

Exhibit 1. Performance of Bass's Model for Selected Durable Goods

	Time of Peak (years)		Magnitude of Peak (thousands of units)	
	Predicted	Actual	Predicted	Actual
Boat Trailers	9.8	10	205	206
Color TVs	6	8	5733	5490
Black and White TVs	7.8	7	7500	7800
Home Freezers	11.6	13	1200	1200
Water Softeners	8.9	9	500	500
Clothes Dryers	8.1	7	1500	1500
Air Conditioners	8.6	7	1800	1700
Lawn Mowers	10.3	11	4000	4200
Coffee Makers	9	10	4800	4900
Record Players	4.8	5	3800	3700

Source: Adapted from Urban and Hauser (1980), p. 102.

In addition to historical sales, the model requires that the manager estimate the initial probability of trial (probability that innovators will purchase the product early in the introductory stage of the product life cycle) and a diffusion rate parameter (which reflects the influence of positive word-of-mouth communication). Given these two estimates, the sales of the product class at time t, S(t), are estimated by the model as

$$S(t) = p(0)m + [q - p(0)]Y(t) - (q/m)[Y(t)^2],$$

where p(0) = initial probability of trial,
      q = diffusion rate parameter,
      m = number of potential buyers,
and Y(t) = number of people who have bought by time t.

1. Bass's market growth equation has three parts:
    a. $p(0)m$
    b. $[q - p(0)]Y(t)$
    c. $(q/m)[Y(t)^2]$
Interpret each part of the equation.

2. Suppose that, for your durable product, you have estimated diffusion rate parameter at 0.3, initial probability of trial at 0.025, and number of potential buyers at 10 million. What are your forecasted sales levels for the first twelve years of sales of this product class? What are cumulative sales at the end of twelve years? According to your estimates, what percentage of potential buyers will have bought this product by the end of twelve years?

3. How do your estimates of cumulative forecasted sales change as the following parameters are varied?
    a. Diffusion rate parameter
    b. Market potential
    c. Initial probability of trial
Specifically, try diffusion rate parameters of 0.2, 0.4, and 0.5. Reset diffusion rate parameter to 0.3, and try a couple of different levels of market potential. Then reset market potential to its original value, and try a couple of levels for initial probability. Graph the resulting sales diffusion patterns.

4. Explain your graphed results for Question 3. Why do the graphs you plotted behave as they do?

Diffusion rate parameter (estimate):   0.3<<
Number of potential buyers of the product: 10000000<<
Initial probability of trial: 0.025<<

MACRO COMMANDS PROVIDED:
(Alt)C: To change parameter estimates.
(Alt)G: To save PrintGraph file (plot of annual sales vs. time).
(Alt)P: To print screen.

File Name: ADVENTUR (Requires LOTUS Release 2.0 or higher)

2.3 THE ADVENTURE PARK, INC.

The Adventure Park is a popular amusement park in a southern state. Within a hundred-mile radius are a number of other tourist attractions such as theme parks, resorts, and famous cities. The park was opened twenty-five years ago.

You have been called upon to prepare a two-year forecast of attendance at Adventure Park. You believe that a straight line regression forecast will be appropriate. You believe that some or all of the following variables are likely to be important determinants of park attendance:
    a. Number of years since the park's opening (to account for attendance growth through time)
    b. Last year's attendance
    c. Oil prices (The majority of park visitors drive there, so, in periods of rising oil prices, traffic to the park is down.)
    d. Whether competing attractions have special events

You expect that rising oil prices would have a detrimental effect upon park attendance. It is less clear how competing attractions will affect Adventure Park's attendance, if at all. Possibly, if a special event is held at a nearby theme park, tourist draw to the region will increase, benefitting Adventure Park and all other parks in the area. Conversely, the competing attraction could divert tourists who otherwise would have visited Adventure Park.

You have gathered the attendance data from Year 1 of operation through last year. You have also obtained oil prices (in index form, where 1.00 = price of oil in Year 1; all prices adjusted for inflation) and a list of major events occurring at neighboring theme parks over the last twenty-five years. For example, in Year 7, a multi-million theme park was built fifty miles away, and an extensive promotional campaign was launched to draw tourists to the area. In Year 11, a nearby city hosted a World's Exhibition. To represent these and similar events, you use a dummy variable: 1 if a major event took place, and 0 otherwise.

You do not know which (if any) of these variables should be in your regression model, so you will investigate a number of combinations to determine which model you should use for forecasting.

1. Using the LOTUS regression procedure, determine attendance as a function of the year number. What is the regression equation? What is the coefficient of determination (R-squared)? Be sure you show that you know how to interpret R-squared.

2. Determine attendance as a function of year number and last

year's attendance. What is the regression equation? How much has R-squared improved?

3. Add oil price index to the model of Question 2. What is the regression equation? How much does this improve R squared?

4. Add the dummy variable for major events to the model of Question 3. What is the regression equation? How much does this improve R squared?

5. Choose one of these regression models to use in forecasting attendance. Explain your choice. Interpret the regression results. What are your attendance projections for Years 26 and 27? In making your projections, assume that oil price index will remain constant at 1.9 for the foreseeable future.

MACRO COMMANDS PROVIDED:

(Alt)I: For instructions on regression.
(Alt)G: To save PrintGraph file (plot of attendance vs. year).
(Alt)P: To print regression results.

File Name: CURVES (Requires LOTUS Release 2.0 or higher)

2.4 DEVELOPMENT OF A FORECASTING MODEL

You are a product manager working on your marketing plan. One of the critical inputs to your plan is a quarterly forecast of industry unit sales. You have diligently gathered the last six years' worth of industry unit sales by quarter (see Exhibit 1) and, because competitive and other environmental factors have not changed that much recently, you believe a time-series forecasting model will be adequate.

You know that over the last six years the product class first experienced substantial growth in sales. This growth rate has been slowing down as the market reached maturity. As a result, you are not sure if simple straight-line regression will be appropriate, and you wish to try some more advanced regression models. Your assistant knows LOTUS programming, and you have asked him to develop some advanced forecasting models. Given the apparent trend toward market maturity, your assistant has suggested three possible models as alternatives to straight-line regression: a square-root model, a logarithmic-function model, and a logistic-function model. For comparison purposes, Exhibit 2 shows what each of these models might look like and also provides the corresponding equation.

Exhibit 1. Industry Unit Sales History

Quarter	Unit Sales (000s)	Quarter	Unit Sales (000s)
1	11	13	129
2	12	14	134
3	13	15	135
4	25	16	139
5	35	17	140
6	40	18	141
7	52	19	139
8	79	20	139
9	94	21	146
10	112	22	139
11	119	23	145
12	125	24	146

Exhibit 2. Alternative Regression Models

a) STRAIGHT-LINE MODEL

$Y = AX + B$

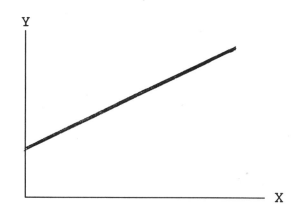

b) SQUARE-ROOT MODEL

$Y = A\sqrt{X} + B$

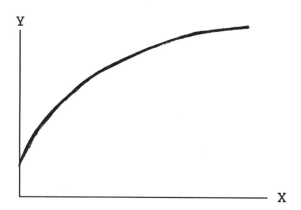

c) LOGARITHMIC-FUNCTION MODEL

$\ln Y = A \ln X + \ln B$

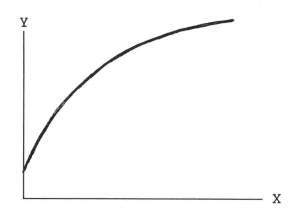

d) LOGISTIC-FUNCTION MODEL

$Y = Y' / (1 + e^{-(AX + B)})$

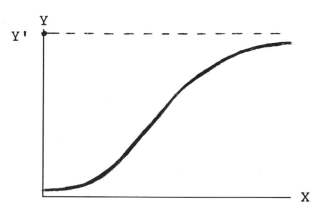

(Note: in the logistic model, Y' is the estimate of market potential. Upon examining Exhibit 1 you have set this at 150,000 units.)

1. Plot the actual (observed) sales figures against time. How would you describe the pattern of industry sales over the last six years?

2. Use regression analysis to find the best straight-line

relationship between quarter and industry sales. Express it as an equation (that is, replace the A and B in the equation above with the slope and Y-intercept). Clearly interpret this equation. Plot sales as estimated by this model against time. Looking at the R squared and standard errors, would you judge this to be a good model?

3. Repeat Question 2 for the square-root model.

4. Repeat Question 2 for the logarithmic-function model.

5. Repeat Question 2 for the logistic-function model.

6. Which of these models would be your best choice for predicting the next three quarters of industry sales? Clearly justify your choice. According to the model you choose, what are the next three quarters of industry sales projected to be?

MACRO COMMANDS PROVIDED:
(Alt)O: To save PrintGraph file of observed sales vs. time.
(Alt)R: To begin a new regression analysis. (Alt)R brings you to a screen where you can choose any of the four models described above.
(Alt)A: To do straight-line model regression.
(Alt)B: To do square-root model regression.
(Alt)C: To do logarithmic-function model regression.
(Alt)D: To do logistic-function model regression.
(Alt)E: To print results of straight-line model regression.
(Alt)F: To print results of square-root model regression.
(Alt)G: To print results of logarithmic-function model regression.
(Alt)H: To print results of logistic-function model regression.

PART 3: PROFITABILITY AND PRODUCTIVITY ANALYSIS

    3.1 Midwest Leather Products (MIDWEST)
    3.2 E-Z Fresh Rug Cleaner (EZFRESH)
    3.3 Gateway Company (GATEWAY)
    3.4 Imperial Camera Shop (IMPERIAL)
    3.5 Top System Carpet Cleaning (TOPSYS)
    3.6 Greenspray, Inc. (GSPRAY)

File Name: MIDWEST

3.1 MIDWEST LEATHER PRODUCTS

Part 1: Contribution Margin Analysis Midwest Leather Products produces and sells leather briefcases and travel bags. The distribution of Midwest products is handled by its own sales force, who call on retail stores. Exhibit 1 below shows the Contribution Margin Statement for Midwest.

Exhibit 1. Midwest Contribution Margin Statement (in $000s)

Retail sales revenue		$2000<<
Less retail margins of 50%		$1000
Manufacturer's sales revenue		$1000
Variable costs for manufacturer		
Var. cost of goods sold	$540<<	
Var. selling costs	$20	
Total variable cost for manufacturer		$560
Var. contribution margin		$440
Fixed costs		
Advertising and sales promotion	$88<<	
Sales salaries and transportation	$58	
Research and development	$12	
General and administrative costs	$30	
Fixed cost of production	$140	
Total fixed cost		$328
Net operating profit before taxes		$112

1. How sensitive is net operating profit before taxes to retail sales revenue? To assess this, try different levels of retail sales revenue, and notice how much net operating profit changes. (Assume retailers maintain their current margins of 50%.)

2. (Reset retail sales revenue to original value.) How sensitive is net operating profit before taxes to changes in fixed costs of advertising and sales promotion? Try values 10% higher and 10% lower than the current advertising and sales promotion cost.

Part 2: Contribution Analysis by Product Line We are not interested only in overall company performance. We also need to examine the performance of each product line, in order to determine its profitability and assess possible marketing strategies for each. To analyze lines of products separately, we have to break down the Contribution Margin Statement by product line. Exhibit 2 gives the Contribution Margin Statement for travel bags and briefcases separately. It is important to note that some of the fixed costs (such as general and administrative costs) are not directly attributable to either of the products; that is, if the company stopped making either travel bags or briefcases, it would still incur these costs. Only the fixed costs <u>directly attributable</u> to one or the other of the products are subtracted from variable contribution margin, to give total contribution to indirect costs and profits.

Exhibit 2: Contribution Margin Statement by Product Line (in $000s)

	Travel Bags	Briefcases
Retail sales revenue	$1200<<	$800<<
Less retail margins	$600	$400
Manufacturer's sales revenue	$600	$400
Var. cost as % of sales	60%<<	50%<<
Tot.var.cost of prodn. & selling	$360	$200
Var. contrib. margin	$240	$200
Direct fixed costs		
Advertising	$32	$16
Sales promotion	$32	$8
Sales force	$8	$8
Transportation	$42	$20
Production	$72	$68
Total direct fixed costs	$166	$120
Total contribution	$74	$80

3. Explain briefly why travel bags provide a lower total contribution, despite the fact that they account for more retail sales revenue.

4. Suppose variable costs were to increase to 65% of sales for travel bags and 55% of sales for briefcases. How would this affect the total contribution of each product line? How would it affect total company profitability?

5. (Reset variable costs as percent of sales to original values.) If you wanted each product to make an $85,000 total contribution to indirect costs and profits, what level of retail sales would be required?

Part 3: P.V.C.M. Exercise   Your spreadsheet shows the percent variable contribution margin (P.V.C.M.) obtained on both product lines. (See Exhibit 3.)

6. Clearly explain the terms "P.V.C.M. on Retail Sales" and "P.V.C.M. on Manufacturer's Sales" in the context of Exhibit 3.

7. How do percent variable contribution margins behave if retail selling prices increase by 10% (assuming retail margins remain at 50%)?

Exhibit 3. Percent Variable Contribution Margins (unit figures in 000s)

	Travel Bags	Briefcases
Units Sold	4000	4000
Retail Selling Price	$300<<	$200<<
Retail Margins	$150	$100
Manuf. Selling Price	$150	$100
Manuf. Var. Cost per Unit	$90	$50
Var. Contr. Margin per Unit	$60	$50
P.V.C.M. on Retail Sales	20%	25%
P.V.C.M. on Manuf. Sales	40%	50%

Part 4: Cost-Volume-Profit Relationships Midwest would like to bring down its average unit costs on briefcases, which currently are $80 per unit. There are two important cost-volume-profit relationships that Midwest can exploit in order to do so:

a. Economies of Scale. If they can produce and sell more briefcases without increasing direct fixed costs, they will spread the fixed costs over a larger number of units. This has the effect of bringing down average total cost per unit.

b. Experience Curve Effects. In addition to scale economies, further reductions in average total cost per unit can occur if Midwest can lower the variable cost per unit. Greater experience with the manufacture of briefcases could reduce waste and inefficiency and cut variable costs. (See Exhibit 4.)

8. First, examine scale economies. If Midwest were able to produce and sell more than 4000 briefcases per year, how would average unit cost be affected? Try several sales levels between 4000 and 8000.

9. Suppose 8000 briefcases were to be produced and sold next year without increasing direct fixed costs. If, on top of scale economies, Midwest could reduce unit variable costs to $46 due to the experience curve, what would average total cost per unit be?

Exhibit 4. Cost-Volume-Profit Relationships for Briefcases

Sales Volume (units)	4000<<
X Unit Variable Cost	$50<<
= Total Variable Cost	$200,000
+ Total Direct Fixed Cost	$120,000
= Total Direct Cost	$320,000
Divided by Volume	4000
= Average Unit Cost	$80

Part 5: Indirect Approach to Budgeting Midwest's objective for the briefcase line next year is to increase that line's total contribution to indirect costs and profit (C.I.C.P.) by $30,000 from current levels. They plan to increase advertising expenditure for briefcases by $20,000. Exhibit 5 shows that, without some increase in current retail sales, current contribution would fall to $60,000 as a result of the new advertising expenses.

10. What level of retail sales revenue would Midwest's briefcase line have to generate in order for the current level of total contribution to be <u>maintained</u>?

11. What level of retail sales revenue would be required for Midwest to meet its objective of increasing total contribution by $30,000?

Exhibit 5. Current and Projected Contribution Margin Statements for Briefcases (all dollar figures in $000s)

	Current	Projected
Retail sales revenue	$800	$800<<
X P.V.C.M.	25%	25%
Var. contr. margin	$200	$200
Direct fixed costs		
Advertising	$14	$36
Sales promotion	$8	$8
Sales force	$8	$8
Transportation	$20	$20
Production	$68	$68
Total direct fixed costs	$120	$140
Total contribution	$80	$60

MACRO COMMANDS PROVIDED:
(Alt)P,Q,R,S,T: To print Parts 1 through 5 of the spreadsheet.
(Alt)I: For a short tutorial on P.V.C.M.
(Alt)C: To change units sold and variable cost levels in Part 4.

<u>Note</u>: This case was developed with the assistance of Prof. Roger J. Calantone of the University of Kentucky and is based on the Midwest Leather Products example in Guiltinan and Paul's first edition, Chapter 5.

File Name: EZFRESH

3.2 E-Z FRESH RUG CLEANER

E-Z Fresh Rug Cleaner has been on the market for about eight years and has achieved a 20% share of the market by 1987. Industry sales were 30 million units in 1987 and are expected to grow by 200,000 units per year in the near future.

Retail price for E-Z Fresh has been unchanged at its current level of $1.75 per unit over the past six years. However, the advertising budget has been gradually increased, reaching $1.4 million in 1987. (In addition to the advertising, other direct costs totaled $1 million.) In 1987, the manufacturer's selling price (to retailers) was $1.25, and manufacturers earned a variable contribution of $0.70 per unit sold. In developing the 1988 budget, the product manager plans to increase advertising by $1.5 million and to increase the retail price (to $1.90) and the manufacturer's price (to $1.50), in order to increase the total contribution to indirect costs and profit by $800,000.

1. What is the current (1987) percent variable contribution margin (P.V.C.M.)? How does it change in 1988?

2. What market share is required to reach the new target contribution?

3. How would the required market share be affected if variable costs of production increased?

4. The product manager has noticed that during the past eight years, each additional $100,000 spent on advertising was accompanied by a 100,000 unit increase in sales. What difficulties might the manager encounter in using this historical advertising-sales relationship to project the sales effects of the new budget?

Exhibit 1. E-Z Fresh Contribution Analysis

	1987	Change	1988
Industry sales	30,000,000	200,000	30,200,000
Market share	20.00%		20.00%<<
Units sold/projected	6,000,000		6,040,000
Retail price	$1.75	$0.15	$1.90
Manufacturer's price	$1.25	$0.25	$1.50
Retailer's margin	$0.50	($0.10)	$0.40
Manuf. var. prodn. costs	$0.55	$0.00	$0.55<<
Var. contrib. mgn.	$0.70	$0.25	$0.95
Total var. contrib.	$4,200,000		$5,738,000
Fixed costs: Adv.	$1,400,000	$1,500,000	$2,900,000
Other	$1,000,000	$0	$1,000,000
Total fixed costs	$2,400,000		$3,900,000
Total contribution	$1,800,000	$38,000	$1,838,000

MACRO COMMAND PROVIDED:
(Alt)P: To print screen.

<u>Note</u>: This problem is based on the Fuzz Fresh case in Guiltinan and Paul's second edition manual.

File Name: GATEWAY

3.3 GATEWAY COMPANY

Gateway Company is a Midwestern publishing house specializing in popular hardcover books. They are about to launch a new novel and require a breakeven analysis on this new book. The book will be sold to booksellers at a tentative price of $22.50 and supported by an advertising and sales promotion campaign that will cost $900,000. The company faces a unit variable cost of $14.00, which includes production, variable selling costs, and all other incurred variable costs. Direct fixed costs, other than advertising and promotion, are projected at $1,250,000. (For a full contribution statement, see Exhibit 1.)

1. What level of unit sales is required for this new book to break even? What level is required for the book to make a contribution to indirect costs and profits of $500,000? Plot a graph showing sales and costs, and locate the breakeven sales level.

2. How would your answer to Question 1 change if any of the following occurred?
    a. Manufacturer's selling price was reduced to $19.00
    b. Variable costs increased by 10%
    c. Additional advertising expenses of $200,000 were incurred
(Test each one individually, and reset to original levels before going on to the next.) In each case, show how P.V.C.M. changes, and also plot a graph showing the new breakeven point.

Exhibit 1. Gateway Company Contribution Margin Statement

	Per Unit	Total	Percent
Units sold	100,000<<		
Manuf. sales	$22.50<<	$2,250,000	
Variable costs	$14.00<<	$1,400,000	
Var. contr. mgn.		$850,000	37.78%
Direct fixed costs			
Adv. & promo.		$900,000<<	
Others		$1,250,000	
Total D.F.C.		$2,150,000	
C.I.C.P.		($1,300,000)	

MACRO COMMANDS PROVIDED:
(Alt)C: To change estimates as indicated in Exhibit 1.
(Alt)G: To save PrintGraph file (plot of sales and cost curves).
(Alt)P: To print screen.

File Name: IMPERIAL

3.4 IMPERIAL CAMERA SHOP

The Imperial Camera Shop is a small local retailer, selling a limited line of cameras and accessories. You have been newly appointed manager and are considering ways to increase the shop's profitability. You believe that reducing price on your main line of 35mm cameras will stimulate additional store traffic and result in higher profit margins, and you want to assess the profit impact of this price reduction.

To understand the full impact of the price reduction, you must remember that a price cut on 35mm cameras will have several additional effects. If more customers are buying expensive cameras, you expect you will sell more flash units and more camera lenses. In addition, with 35mm cameras at a sufficiently low price, some individuals who might have bought an inexpensive instant camera might trade up and buy a better 35mm camera. An economist would characterize the flash units and lenses as complementary goods, and the instant cameras as a substitute good. Thus, your impact analysis must consider the cross-impacts of a 35mm camera price change on demand for these complementary and substitute goods.

You have built a LOTUS spreadsheet of your shop's annual contribution margin analysis (see Exhibit 1). It reflects current prices, costs, and sales levels. By looking at the historical price and sales data for your product lines, you determine the following:

a. Decreasing the 35mm camera selling price by $50 would stimulate the sale of about 100 additional 35mm cameras per year. This move would probably decrease annual unit sales of instant cameras by 10% and increase annual unit sales of flash units and lenses by 10% each.

b. Lowering the 35mm camera selling price by $100 would increase the projected sale of 35mm cameras by about 150 units. Instant camera sales would decrease by 20%, and sales of complementary goods would increase by 20%.

c. Lowering the 35mm camera selling price by $150 would increase the projected sale of 35mm cameras by about 200 units. Instant camera sales would decrease by 30%, and sales of complementary goods would increase by 40%.

1. If your objective were to maximize pre-tax profit, which of the three proposed price reductions would you recommend? Or do all of them provide a projected profit level lower than the current level?

2. For the pricing program you choose, discuss how the contributions to indirect costs and profits made by each of the four product lines are affected. (Be more specific than "They increased" or "They decreased." Express your answer in terms of percentage changes, and discuss these.)

3. For the pricing program you choose, how sensitive is your shop's pre-tax profit to increases in the variable costs you incur in handling the 35mm cameras? Try variable cost levels 10% and 20% higher than current levels.

Exhibit 1. Imperial Camera Shop Annual Contribution Statement

	35mm Cameras	Instant Cameras	Flash Units	Lenses	Total
Unit sales	200<<	300<<	150<<	100<<	
Sell. price	$599<<	$199	$89	$199	
Var. costs	$300<<	$80	$60	$140	
P.V.C.M.	49.92%	59.80%	32.58%	29.65%	
V.Contr. Mgn.	$299	$119	$29	$59	
$ Var. contr.	$59800	$35700	$4350	$5900	$105,750
Dir.f.costs	$25000	$22500	$2000	$3000	$52,500
C.I.C.P.	$34800	$13200	$2350	$2900	$53,250
Indir.f.costs					$38,000
Pre-tax profit					$15,250

MACRO COMMANDS PROVIDED:
(Alt)S: To change sales figures for each product line.
(Alt)C: To change price or variable cost of 35mm camera.
(Alt)P: To print screen.

File Name: TOPSYS

3.5 TOP SYSTEM CARPET CLEANING

Top System provides carpet cleaning services to residents of a Northeastern community of 600,000 people. Last year, a total of 10,000 homeowners had their carpets cleaned by Top System, at an average price of $40. (The actual charge to the homeowner was variable and depended upon the extent of the required cleaning.) Variable costs incurred by Top System were about 50% of sales revenue. Last year, $40,000 was invested in advertising. Other fixed costs amounted to $80,000.

Top System concentrates its efforts on the homeowner market. Although a lucrative market in cleaning carpets in offices, hotels, and motels exists in this city, large competitors account for nearly 100% of this business and have done so for many years.

The homeowner market is quite seasonal. Typically, a substantial proportion of carpet cleaning revenues occur during the spring cleaning months of March, April, and May. The summer months of June, July, and August also account for a high percentage of yearly revenues, as homeowners are cleaning up for visitors or opening their summer cottages. The remaining six months (September through February) usually are the slow period. Last year was no exception: Of the 10,000 contracts Top System obtained, 4500 were during the spring, 3200 during the summer, and 2300 during the fall and winter months combined.

Of the $40,000 invested in advertising last year, $18,000 was spent during the spring, $12,000 during the summer, and $10,000 during fall and winter. The owner of the company, Jim Smith, was concerned that his variable costs were going to increase over the next year from 50% to 60% of sales, mostly due to rising materials costs. Because there were many large competitors and price competition was rather fierce, he felt it would be unwise to increase prices to offset the loss in contribution. Thus, he decided to increase advertising. Specifically, he was planning on increases of $8000 in the spring and $4000 in the summer.

At this point, Mr. Smith showed his advertising budget plans to his wife, Susan, who was Senior Vice President of Accounts with one of the nation's top three advertising agencies. (They met while he was a senior and she was a sophomore at a nearby business school.) She immediately wanted to know where the proposed budget increases came from. At first, he tried to rationalize them from a profitability standpoint ("We don't want to spend too little on advertising, but it can get quite expensive and the chance of overspending is high"), but he finally had to admit that they came out of thin air.

Mrs. Smith asked him if he remembered the ADBUDG model from the Marketing Strategy and Planning course, but it became apparent that he could hardly remember even taking the course. Since historical data weren't readily available and there was little time to conduct any experiments, she suggested he should try to formalize his subjective judgments. Without even referring to her textbook, she developed six questions for him to answer:

1. How many potential customers are there for your business in each of the three periods?
2. If you had unlimited funds for advertising, what is the maximum share of potential customers you would obtain in each period (considering likely competitive retaliation)?
3. If advertising were cut to zero, what is the minimum share of potential customers you would obtain in each period?
4. What level of expenditure is needed in each period to retain the previous year's market share?
5. If advertising expenditures were increased by 50% in each period, what would be your estimate of the market share you would obtain?
6. What share of potential customers would be obtained in each period if you simply repeated last year's advertising plan?

Exhibit 1 gives Mr. Smith's responses to these questions. For more information on the ADBUDG model, see Little's article "Models and Managers: The Concept of a Decision Calculus" in *Management Science*, April 1970.

Mrs. Smith loaded these answers into the ADBUDG spreadsheet program that she had written herself on her personal computer. She was then able to determine what the impact would be of different advertising budgets on market share and sales for each period. Since she also had cost data, she could determine effects on profits as well. Thus, she could develop a marketing budget for Top System for next year.

1. Given Mr. Smith's proposed increase in the advertising budget and no changes in other direct costs, what sales volume is required next year to achieve a target contribution (C.I.C.P.) of $90,000? (Do this calculation by hand.)

2. Using the ADBUDG model and Mr. Smith's ADBUDG estimates, determine the advertising budget levels for the three periods that yield the greatest total contribution for next year. (Do this by changing figures as indicated in Exhibit 2. HINT: Once you have found the best budget for spring, move on to summer, then do fall and winter.)

3. Suppose Mr. Smith's estimates of maximum shares were changed to 40%, 38% and 32% for the three periods, and the estimates of the "plus-50" shares were changed to 36%, 34% and 30%. How would this change your answer to Question 2?

Exhibit 1. Mr. Smith's ADBUDG Estimates

	Spring	Summer	Fall-Winter
Potential customers	15,000	12,800	10,000
Max. share with saturation advertising	50%<<	36%<<	28%<<
Min. share with no advertising	10%	5%	5%
Share with 50% increase in adv.	38%<<	33%<<	26%<<
Last year's share	30%	25%	23%
Budget needed to maintain current share	18,000	12,000	10,000

Exhibit 2. Seasonal Analysis

	Spring	Summer	Fall-Winter	Total
Advertising budget	$18000<<	$12000<<	$10000<<	$40000
Projected share	30%	25%	23%	
Projected sales	180000	128000	92000	400000
Projected V.C.M.	90000	64000	46000	200000
Fixed costs				
Advertising				40000
Other				80000
Total fixed costs				120000
Total contribution				80000

MACRO COMMANDS PROVIDED:
(Alt)G: To save PrintGraph file of (approximate) ADBUDG curves
    (for Spring, Summer, or Fall-Winter).
(Alt)P: To print results.

File Name: GSPRAY

3.6 GREENSPRAY, INC.

Greenspray provides lawn fertilizing and weed control services to homeowners in a community of 300,000 people. During the spring and summer of 1988, the company had contracts with 6,000 homeowners, with the average contract amount being $150. Variable costs averaged 50% of sales; advertising costs were $45,000; and other direct costs totalled $300,000 during 1988. In addition to its regular fertilizing and weed control services, Greenspray also offered a special fall service, thatching and seeding, at an average price of $80. In 1988, 500 homeowners purchased this service. (Variable costs for the fall service were approximately 50% of the price of the service.)

Greenspray faces two very strong competitors in this market, both of whom can be counted on to react strongly to any competitive pressures. In this highly competitive market, Greenspray had a 25% share of the lawn services market in this community from January to April and a 12.5% share from May to June. They also had 25% of the fall thatching and seeding business in the community.

In 1988, Greenspray spent $30,000 in advertising during the January-April period, $10,000 in May and June, and $5,000 in the fall (August and September). As 1989 approached, the company's owner was faced with several problems. The cost of material and of gasoline for the company's trucks was rapidly rising. At the same time, competitive price pressures made it difficult to increase prices. As a consequence, the percent variable contribution margin was expected to fall to 40% in 1989. To offset this profit squeeze, the owner had decided that an increase in advertising was necessary. Specifically, he planned on increases of $15,000 in May-June and $3,000 in the fall. Before the owner's plans were finalized, he showed them to his daughter, a marketing student who had just finished her fall semester. After reviewing the plans, she asked him what assumptions he had used to develop the budget figures.

"Well, my advertising agency just computed the cost of the basic programs for me," he replied. "Of course, I could expand the April advertising campaign or the May and June campaign. And we could expand the Fall campaign as well, to reach more customers. But advertising and personal selling can get awfully expensive. I know that sales will fall off if we cut our promotional budget. But I also believe that you can spend more than is worthwhile from a profitability standpoint."

Recognizing that her father had little in the way of historical data and had no time to conduct any experiments, the daughter suggested that he try to formalize his subjective judgments. Specifically, she asked him to write down the following information for each of the three promotional periods.

a. Based on his knowledge of the local market and past sales data, how many potential customers are there for the fertilizing and weed control services, and how many of these customers are likely to make a decision in January-April versus in May-June?

b. How many potential customers are there for the fall service?

c. If he had unlimited funds for advertising and promotion, what is the maximum share of potential customers he could obtain (after considering competition, the state of the local economy, and local lawn conditions) in each period?

d. If advertising and selling were cut to zero, what is the minimum share of potential customers he would obtain in each period?

e. What level of expenditures is needed in each period to retain the share of market he held last year?

f. If promotional expenditures were increased by 50% in each period, what would be his best estimate of the market share he would obtain in each period?

g. What share of potential customers would be obtained in each period if he simply repeated last year's promotional plan?

Given this information, the daughter had all the data needed to use an ADBUDG model, which would enable her to examine the impact of different budget levels for each period on Greenspray's share of company potential and thus on Greenspray sales. Additionally, given the cost data for Greenspray, she would be able to examine the profit implications of different budget levels. She could thus develop a marketing budget for Greenspray for 1989. (For information on the ADBUDG model, see Little's article "Models and Managers: The Concept of a Decision Calculus" in *Management Science*, April 1970.)

1. Given the proposed increase in the advertising budget and no change in other direct costs, what sales volume is required in 1989 in order to achieve a target contribution of $100,000? (Calculate this by hand; remember P.V.C.M. is expected to decline to 40%.)

2. Play the role of the Greenspray manager. For each season, select the levels of the ADBUDG model parameters (i.e., maximum share, minimum share, reference advertising level) that you think would apply. (See Exhibit 1.) Explain the reasoning behind each parameter you select.

3. Using the ADBUDG model and your estimates in Question 2,

determine the budget levels for the three periods that yield the greatest total contribution for the year 1989, by varying advertising budgets as shown in Exhibit 2.

4. Suppose your estimates of the maximum shares were increased by 3% for each of the three periods and your estimates of the "plus-50" shares were increased by 2%.
    a. How would this change the answer to Question 3?
    b. If you felt that both sets of maximum and plus-50 share estimates were equally likely, how should you proceed in terms of your budgeting decision?

5. What product objectives (in terms of market share and profitability) do you think are appropriate for Greenspray?

Exhibit 1. Spreadsheet for ADBUDG Estimates

	Jan.-Apr.	May-June	Fall
Potential customers:	20000	8000	2000
1988 share:	25%	12.5%	25%
Dollars needed to maintain current share:	$0<<	$0<<	$0<<
Maximum share given saturation advertising:	0%<<	0%<<	0%<<
Minimum share with no advertising:	0%<<	0%<<	0%<<
Share with 50% increase in advertising:	0%<<	0%<<	0%<<

Exhibit 2. Seasonal Analysis

	Jan.-Apr.	May-June	Fall	Total
Adv. budget:	$30000<<	$10000<<	$5000<<	$45000
Projected share:	25%	12.5%	25%	
Projected sales level:	$750000	$150000	$40000	$940000
Projected VCM:	$300000	$ 60000	$16000	$376000
Fixed Costs:				
Advertising				$45000
Other				$300000
Total fixed costs:				$345000
Total contribution:				$31000

HINTS FOR GREENSPRAY ADBUDG ESTIMATION

1. You have two very strong competitors. (How will this affect your assessment of maximum possible market share?)

2. You know last year's advertising budgets and resulting market shares.

3. Greenspray is well established, and it is unlikely that cutting advertising to zero would lead to a market share of zero.

Remember there are no right or wrong estimates! But, given the above information, some are more realistic than others.

MACRO COMMANDS PROVIDED:
(Alt)G: To save PrintGraph file of (approximate) ADBUDG curves for January-April, May-June, and Fall.
(Alt)P: To print results.

Note: This problem is based on the Greenspray case in Guiltinan and Paul's second edition manual.

PART 4: PRODUCT PROGRAMS

4.1   Lucas Company (LUCAS)
4.2   Mitchell Stationery Company (MITCHELL)
4.3   Assessor Exercise (ASSESSOR)
4.4   Product Positioning Using Perceptor (PERCEPT)
4.5   Conquer Brand Analgesic (CONQUER)

File Name: LUCAS

4.1 LUCAS COMPANY

The Lucas Company manufactures a wide variety of electronic products in the United States and in Asian subsidiaries. They have been examining possible ways in which they could expand their base of operations and have come up with the idea of entering the computer software market with a series of home entertainment programs. They have the technical capabilities, and they have a well-established distribution channel already available that could handle this product. It would require, however, substantial investment in plant and equipment in order to mass-market this product. The company is debating whether it would be worthwhile to launch this product nationwide. To assist in making this decision, Lucas top management requested projected profit and loss statements for the first five years of the product's life (from 1988 to 1992). These statements appear in Exhibit 1.

The investment required this year to bring the product to market is assessed at $7 million, of which $6 million is investment in plant and equipment, and $1 million is startup cost of production and marketing. Straight-line depreciation over five years will be used in accounting for the plant and equipment costs. Industry sales forecasts for this market are projected as appear in the statements, and Lucas expects that they can capture 9% of the market in Year 1, with increases to 10% by Year 3. Lucas's selling price will be set at $50, and based on experience with similar products, Lucas expects a 25% variable contribution margin on sales. Direct expenses are forecasted as appear in the statements, and the tax rate is 46%. The company has set a minimum rate of return of 28%.

1. What is the net present value (NPV) of the project?

2. What is the payback period? (Calculate by hand.)

3. How would NPV be affected if each of the following situations occurred? (Test each situation individually, resetting to original levels before going on to the next.)
    a. if expected market share reached 9% in the first year but then stayed constant at 9% (did not increase as expected).
    b. if selling price had to be cut to $40 in 1990 due to competitive pressure and then maintained at $40 for 1991 and 1992.
    c. if direct fixed expenses were $500,000 higher than projected for each of the five years.

4. Lucas management believes that there is about a 20% chance that any one of these negative situations may occur. They assess the

probability that <u>all three</u> would occur at about 1%. How would NPV be affected if <u>all three</u> situations occurred?

5. Would you make the recommendation to introduce the product? Explain clearly.

Exhibit 1. Lucas Company Profit and Loss Statement (dollar figures in millions)

	1988	1989	1990	1991	1992
Ind. Sales Forecast	15.00	15.75	16.54	17.36	18.23
X Exp. Mkt. Share	9%	9%	10%<<	10%<<	10%<<
Unit Sales (Mill.)	1.35	1.42	1.65	1.74	1.82
X Selling Price	$50	$50	$50<<	$50<<	$50<<
Sales Revenue	67.50	70.88	82.69	86.82	91.16
VCM (25% of sales)	16.88	17.72	20.67	21.71	22.79
- Direct Exp.	13.50<<	13.00<<	12.50<<	12.00<<	12.00<<
- Depreciation	1.20	1.20	1.20	1.20	1.20
Earn. Before Tax	2.18	3.52	6.97	8.51	9.59
- Tax (46% Earn.)	1.00	1.62	3.21	3.91	4.41
Earn. After Tax	1.17	1.90	3.76	4.59	5.18
+ Depreciation	1.20	1.20	1.20	1.20	1.20
Annual Cash Flow	2.37	3.10	4.96	5.79	6.38
NPV of Cash Inflow	1.86	1.89	2.37	2.16	1.86

MACRO COMMAND PROVIDED:
(Alt)P: To print screen.

4.2 MITCHELL STATIONERY COMPANY

Mitchell Stationery Company sells numerous stationery products including a small yearly appointment book. The book is forecasted to capture 6% of the total market of 35 million units next year: that is, expected sales are 2,100,000 units. Of this amount, 45%, or 945,000 units, are expected to be sold to repeat customers, with the remainder being sold to individuals who bought a competing book (or no book at all) last year. The book sells for $1.20, with an $0.80 gross margin per unit, giving a $1,680,000 forecasted gross margin for next year. Marketing expenditures and overhead are budgeted at $800,000, so the product is expected to provide a before-tax profit of $880,000 and a return on investment (ROI) of 22%.

A new, more compact appointment book has been designed, and Mitchell must decide whether the new book should be launched for the next calendar year. It satisfies some, but not all, buyer needs. The compact size makes it easy to fit in a pocket or purse, but, since it has fewer pages and a smaller size, some individuals may find it inadequate. It is tentatively priced at $0.90, and gross margin per unit is projected at $0.60. The benefits of lower price and small size are expected to boost overall sales of the product category (appointment books) to 45 million units. Taken together, both products are expected to obtain 10% of appointment book sales, for a total of 4,500,000 units. Marketing expenditures and overhead allocated to the new product are set at $900,000. Some, but not all, sales of the new book are projected to be cannibalized from the sales of the existing product. The amount of cannibalization is projected by top management to be 1 million units.

1. Assuming the projections given above are reasonable, what would the effect on company profits and return on investment be if the new book is introduced? How is this figure affected when cannibalization of existing product sales is taken into account?

2. What market share would have to be achieved to offset the effects of cannibalization (i.e., increase revised ROI to 22%)?

3. Test the sensitivity of profit and ROI to each of the following conditions. (Try them one at a time; remember to reset to original levels before proceeding to the next.)
    a. if total market units were overestimated by 10%; underestimated by 10%.
    b. if actual company market share were 6%; 8%; 12%; 14%.
    c. if the number of cannibalized customers were higher than projected; lower than projected.

      d. if unit price of the new product had to be lowered to $0.80 due to competitive pressure.
      e. if marketing expenses and overhead had been underestimated.

4. Aside from increased profitability, what other reasons might Mitchell have for launching a new product that is expected to cannibalize sales of existing products?

Exhibit 1. Profit Analysis for Mitchell Stationery Company

	Current Product	New Product	Combined
Fcst. total market units			45000000<<
Fcst. market share			0.10<<
Fcst. unit volume			4500000
Source of volume:			
New customers	0	1965000	1965000
Competitors' cust.	300000	435000	735000
Cannibalized cust.	0	1000000<<	1000000
Repeat customers	800000	0	800000
Total customers	1100000	3400000	4500000
Market share	2.4%	7.6%	10.0%
Unit price	$1.20	$0.90<<	
Total revenue	$1,320,000	$3,060,000	$4,380,000
Gross margin/unit	$0.80	$0.60	
Gross margin ($)	$880,000	$2,040,000	$2,920,000
Mkt. exp. + overhead	$800,000	$900,000<<	$1,700,000
Profit before tax	$80,000	$1,140,000	$1,220,000

MACRO COMMAND PROVIDED:
(Alt)P: To print profit analysis, either before or after launch of new product.

<u>Note</u>: This case was developed with the assistance of Prof. Roger J. Calantone of the University of Kentucky.

File Name: ASSESSOR

4.3 ASSESSOR EXERCISE

ASSESSOR is a pre-test market model, originally designed by Silk and Urban (1978). Pre-test market models give projections of long-run market share for a new product before it is test marketed. The method is made available to new product planners through market research firms and is substantially cheaper to apply than a full-scale test market. It also usually produces results in three or four months, which is about one third the time span of a typical test market. The results of a pre-test market may be so favorable that it would be better for the company to skip test marketing altogether and save the cost. In other cases, the results may be sufficiently poor to indicate that the product should be dropped before the test marketing stage.

ASSESSOR uses relatively easily obtainable data (such as satisfaction ratings, use rates, likelihood of repeat purchases, brand ratings) to assess long-run market share.

We shall look at a simplified version of ASSESSOR. In it, ultimate market share is related to penetration rate and repeat rate:

$$S = P \times R$$

where S = ultimate market share,
P = ultimate penetration rate (long-run trial),
and R = ultimate repeat rate among those who try the brand.

Penetration rate P of a new brand is related to the amount of advertising and sales promotion (sampling) that the company does. It is expressed as:

$$P = F \times K \times D + C \times U - (F \times K \times D) \times (C \times U)$$

where F = long-run probability of trial given unlimited distribution and awareness,
K = long-run probability of awareness,
D = long-run probability of availability,
C = probability of the consumer receiving a free sample, and
U = probability that a consumer receiving a free sample will use it.

The equation for penetration is thus made up of one part representing advertising effects ($F \times K \times D$), one part representing sampling effects ($C \times U$), and a third part to subtract those individuals who were counted twice.

The equation for repeat rate R is more complex and shows R to be related to q(k,z), the probability that a consumer who purchased product k last period will switch to the new brand z this period, and to q(z,z), the probability that someone who bought the new brand last period will buy it again this period. The accompanying computer program gives more details on this second equation.

Now that we have P and R, we can multiply them to obtain the projected long-run market share S.

The accompanying spreadsheet (see Exhibit 1) provides estimates of all the parameters needed to estimate P and R, obtained through questionnaires, followup phone surveys, and managerial judgment. It also shows some other data required to perform the analysis: The brand's projected price and unit variable cost are $5.00 and $2.40, respectively; industry sales volume is estimated at 10 million units per year; and estimated direct fixed costs are as follows:
    Advertising: $3,000,000.
    Sales Promotion: $1,500,000.
    Other: $1,000,000.

1. Assess the long-run market share for this brand based on these parameters. At this market share, what is your assessment of the brand's long-run profitability?

2. Test the sensitivity of projected long-run market share and profitability to changes in C, U, q(z,z), q(k,z), F, K, and D. Which of these are the most crucial variables (in that a small error will lead to great changes in estimated market share)?

3. Your best market information indicates that if you increased the proposed advertising budget to $4,000,000, long-run awareness would increase to 90%. Would increasing the advertising to this level be worth it, in terms of increasing long-run profitability?

4. (Set advertising budget and long-run awareness back to original levels.) Your promotional department discovered that if you double your sales promotion expenditure, you could increase the average customer's probability of receiving a sample to 40%. Would this high level of sales promotion be worth it, in terms of increasing long-run profitability?

5. What would happen to long-run profitability if you increased both advertising and sales promotion as described in Questions 3 and 4?

Exhibit 1. ASSESSOR Spreadsheet

```
   ---Parameter Values---
Prob. of switching to new brand      q(k,z):         0.6 <<
Prob. of repurchasing new brand      q(z,z):         0.55<<
Long-run trial probability              F:           0.7 <<
Advertising expenditures              ADV:    $3,000,000<<
Long-run awareness probability          K:           0.8 <<
Long-run availability probability       D:           0.75<<
Sales promotion expenditures           SP:    $1,500,000<<
Prob. of receiving a sample             C:           0.25<<
Prob. of trying a received sample       U:           0.6 <<

   ---Calculated Values---
Ultimate penetration rate               P:           0.51
Ultimate repeat rate                    R:           0.57
Ultimate long-run market share          S:          28.97%
Ultimate long-run profitability        PR:    $2,032,571
```

MACRO COMMAND PROVIDED:
(Alt)P: To print main screen.

File Name: PERCEPT

4.4 PRODUCT POSITIONING USING THE PERCEPTOR MODEL

You are the newly-appointed manager of the Quality Motor Company's Truck Division. Your job is to secure a competitive position for Quality in the light truck market which has traditionally been dominated by three major competitors: A, B and C. The automotive engineers and designers have developed a couple of tentative designs, and top management is keen on moving one of these to the prototype stage. Your task is to assess which of these designs has the better chance of sustaining a strong long-run market share in this very competitive industry.

A customer questionnaire was issued to owners and prospective buyers of light trucks, both for commercial and private use. The questionnaire was designed to determine perceptions and preferences in light truck purchases. It was determined through factor analysis of the questionnaire results that there are two major attributes upon which light trucks are assessed by the average buyer: economy in gas mileage and sporty style.

The questionnaire results were used to construct a positioning map that shows the average customer's rating of each make of truck on each of the two dimensions. The map also indicates the ideal point: the combination of economy and sportiness that would be preferred by the average customer if it were available. On the whole, customers prefer a truck that is a little on the sporty side (but not too sporty) and are willing to forego some economy to get this. Of course there are some customers who want other combinations of sportiness and economy, but on average the ideal point indicated represents the wants of the market as a whole. The map appears in Exhibit 1. The map indicates the two designs that have been developed by Quality: these are M, at point (4,4), and N, at point (-1,-1).

You believe that the PERCEPTOR model provides accurate projections of long-run market share for this industry. The accompanying computer program gives details on the PERCEPTOR model. Briefly, it takes the positions of existing and proposed brands, as well as the ideal point, and determines long-run market shares based on squared distances from the ideal, managerial assessment of awareness and availability of brand, and probabilities of trial and repeat purchase. Note: for information on PERCEPTOR and its trial-repeat structure, see the Urban (1975) and Parfitt and Collins (1969) references listed at the end of this book. PERCEPTOR also shows from which brands the new brand draws its share (that is, it estimates the loss in share to new brand from each of the old brands). Long-run awareness for the new light truck is assessed by management to be 90%, and the long-run availability is 85%.

Exhibit 1. Positioning Map

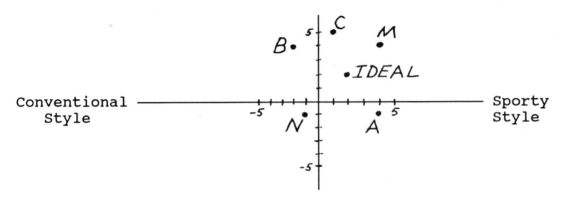

For each design M and N, find:
a. squared distance of new make from ideal,
b. ultimate probability of trial of new make, given awareness and availability,
c. long-run share of purchases among those who have ever tried the new make,
d. long-run market share,
e. estimated loss in long-run share to new make from each of the three existing makes.

2. Choose two other positionings for the new make (not on the ideal point!), and determine the same items as you did for Question 1.

3. Of the four positionings you have assessed, which would you recommend to move on to the prototype construction stage? Why?

4. Suppose that a number of new dealers could be recruited to handle the new truck so that more market areas could be covered. This move boosts long-run availability to 90%. How does this affect the long-run market share and the estimated losses in shares for the positioning you recommended in Question 3?

5. Suppose that the advertising campaign developed for the new make is insufficient (for example, competition for the light truck market could get extremely fierce, and A, B and C all increase their advertising budgets substantially). If you could achieve a long-run awareness level of only 75%, how would that affect long-run market share and the estimated losses in shares?

Exhibit 2. PERCEPTOR Data

	X-coord.	Y-coord.
New Brand's Position	5<<	2<<
Ideal Brand's Position	2	2
Brand A's Position	4	-1
Brand B's Position	-2	4
Brand C's Position	1	5

Squared distance of new brand from ideal:	9
Long-run market share:	0.453
Sources of new brand share:	
From Brand A:	0.285
From Brand B:	0.054
From Brand C:	0.114
Ultimate probability of trial of new brand given awareness and availability:	0.888
Long-run Awareness:	0.900<<
Long-run Availability:	0.850<<
Fraction of target market that ever tries new brand:	0.679
Long-run share of purchases among those who have ever tried brand:	0.667
Long-run market share:	0.453

MACRO COMMANDS PROVIDED:
(Alt)G: To save PrintGraph file of positioning map.
(Alt)C: To make changes to new brand coordinates, awareness, or availability.
(Alt)P: To print main screen.

File Name: CONQUER

4.5 CONQUER BRAND ANALGESIC

You work for a national pharmaceutical company that manufactures a brand of pain reliever (analgesic) known as Conquer. The pain reliever market is characterized by stiff competition; Conquer is currently the number four brand with 15.78% of the market. Exhibit 1 provides current market shares for Conquer and the three major competitors.

This market has been exhaustively analyzed by your marketing research department. Through extensive questioning and data analysis, they determined that the two most important attributes to consumers, when choosing a brand of analgesic to purchase, are its gentleness (easy on the stomach and heart) and its efficacy (how quickly and completely it relieves pain). The research also showed that two distinct consumer segments exist in the marketplace. Some consumers seek a gentle pain reliever; they, of course, want it to be effective, but will sacrifice high efficacy in order to get gentleness. Others seek the most effective pain reliever they can find, and gentleness is not that important to them. The ideal brand positions reflect these preferences and are provided in Exhibit 1. Also in Exhibit 1 are the perceived positions of Conquer and its three main competitors, Brands X, Y, and Z. Exhibit 2 represents all the positioning information in a perceptual map.

Looking at the map in Exhibit 2, you can see one of the main problems Conquer faces; its position is not very strong on either attribute. Other brands offer either more gentleness or higher efficacy, and would thus be preferred by consumers. Not coincidentally, the two market share leaders (Brands X and Z) are each perceived as being close to an ideal point: Brand X is the gentlest analgesic yet still quite effective, while Brand Z is the most effective by far. Brand X, in fact, is perceived higher than Conquer on both attributes. Further, you have a competitor (Brand Y) perceived to be very similar to Conquer, which probably further reduces Conquer's market share.

You recognize that repositioning Conquer is a sensible option. But how should you do it? Change its chemical formula so it is as effective as Brand Z? Make it gentler than Brand X? Perhaps Conquer really is more effective and gentler than consumers perceive it to be, and its promotion hasn't been strong enough. Whatever you choose to do, however, you realize it will cost you. As a rule of thumb, costs of repositioning increase more than proportionally, the further it is you move. These repositioning costs are treated as additional fixed costs in the spreadsheet (see Exhibit 1) and increase very rapidly the further you move.

Exhibit 1. Company and Industry Data: Conquer Brand Analgesic

	Attribute 1 (Gentleness)	Attribute 2 (Efficacy)	Market Share (%)
Segment 1 Ideal	4	2	
Segment 2 Ideal	1	4.5	
Conquer	1.2 <<	1.2 <<	15.78%
Brand X	3.2	2.4	31.63%
Brand Y	1 <<	1.25 <<	15.55%
Brand Z	0.7	3.6	37.03%

Projected Conquer Sales (000s of gross)	7,891
Variable Contribution Margin per gross	$100
Dollar Variable Contribution Margin	$789,100
Fixed Costs of Repositioning	0
Other Fixed Costs	$400,000
Total Fixed Costs	$400,000
C.I.C.P.	$389,100

Exhibit 2. Positioning Map

Efficacy

```
    • SEG.2

  Z•

                    • X
                          • SEG.1

  Y•  • CONQUER

                                          Gentleness
```

There are some other factors to keep in mind when repositioning. The closer you are to an ideal point, the more market share you will draw from that point. But remember that both ideal points are relatively well served by existing brands, so it is unrealistic to assume you will be able to draw all of the sales from a segment by repositioning close to it. Also, your competitors can reposition just as well as you, so it is reasonable to assume that a strong attack move on your part will invite competitive retaliation.

1. Try several possible repositioning strategies for Conquer. Would you recommend they move in the direction of Segment 1's ideal point, or Segment 2's? If you were to choose among your repositionings on the basis of maximum contribution to indirect costs and profit, which would you recommend? How much is your market share improved? Which brand(s) would be hurt the most (in terms of lost share) by your repositioning? Plot a positioning map of your recommended course of action.

2. Take the repositioning you recommended in Question 1. Assume that Brand Y will retaliate by repositioning itself to the point (2, 3.5). How does this repositioning affect your market share and your contribution to indirect costs and profit? Plot a positioning map representing this situation.

MACRO COMMANDS PROVIDED:
(Alt)C: To change Conquer's or Brand Y's position.
(Alt)G: To save PrintGraph file of the positioning map.
(Alt)P: To print main screen.

PART 5: PRICING PROGRAMS

5.1 Corbett Company (CORBETT)
5.2 Cost-Plus Pricing Exercise (COSTPLUS)
5.3 National Electric (NATIONAL)
5.4 Eastside Construction Co. (EASTSIDE)
5.5 Business Applications, Inc. (BUSINESS)

File Name: CORBETT

5.1 CORBETT COMPANY

The Corbett Company, manufacturer of confectionery products, is soon to be launching a new candy bar in the national market. They are considering a selling price to distributors of $0.59 each. Best cost estimates indicate that variable costs (including direct labor and materials as well as all other variable costs) will amount to approximately $0.47 per candy bar. Fixed costs of research, advertising and selling, and other direct fixed costs will amount to $270,000. The contribution margin analysis in Exhibit 1 categorizes these costs in greater detail.

1. What is the break-even sales volume for this product? Plot sales and costs against volume and locate the break-even point on your plot.

2. What is the break-even sales volume assuming the company wants to make a minimum profit of $27,000 during the first year? Find this point on your plot.

3. How do your answers to 1 and 2 change if the following occurrences happen? (Try these one at a time, resetting to original value before continuing.) Plot a new break-even analysis for each.
    a. Direct materials costs are forced up to $0.20 by sugar and cocoa suppliers.
    b. Competitors substantially increase advertising budget, and Corbett responds in kind by also increasing budget by 10%.
    c. Price cutting occurs in the industry as competition becomes even more cut-throat, and Corbett responds by lowering price to $0.57.
    d. All three of these events happen at the same time.

4. How would you describe the sensitivity of the break-even point to each of the above events? Which is the most critical determinant of break-even volume?

Exhibit 1. Corbett Company Contribution Analysis

Number of Units Sold (000s)		2250<<	
Selling price		$0.59<<	
Variable costs			
Direct labor	$0.11		
Direct materials	$0.18<<		
Other	$0.18		
Total variable costs		$0.47	
Variable contribution margin		$0.12	$270,000
Direct fixed costs			
Research and development	$60,000		
Advertising and selling	$180,000<<		
Other direct fixed costs	$30,000		
Total direct fixed costs			$270,000
Contribution to indirect costs and profit			$0

MACRO COMMANDS PROVIDED:
(Alt)C: To change estimates in spreadsheet as shown in Exhibit 1.
(Alt)G: To save PrintGraph file of break-even analysis.
(Alt)P: To print main screen.

<u>Note</u>: This case was developed with the assistance of Prof. Roger J. Calantone of the University of Kentucky.

File Name: COSTPLUS

5.2 COST-PLUS PRICING EXERCISE

In cost-plus pricing, we set prices on our products in order to achieve a desired profit target. Working from estimates of unit sales for the next year, we determine total costs per unit and add our desired profit target to arrive at our (manufacturer's) selling price. Dealers add their margin to arrive at the price to the customer.

In this problem we classify variable costs into two groups: materials costs and assembly costs. Materials costs are generally more liquid than assembly costs (which include labor and machine-time costs). They are also usually turned over faster and can be more easily adjusted by management for variation in output. By contrast, assembly costs are less flexible. One cannot hire and lay off workers, or buy and sell off machines, every time there is a small variation in output. Thus, these costs involve a longer-term investment.

Our company makes three products: A, B, and C. The spreadsheet given in Exhibit 1 contains materials and assembly variable costs per unit, estimated sales volume (in units) for the next year, desired profit target (expressed as a percentage of unit costs), and other data.

1. Decrease estimated unit sales by 10% for each product, and compare your results to the original spreadsheet. How is price to customer affected by lower estimated unit sales? Why does price behave this way? Explain the implications of your observation.

2. Suppose you do not want the price of Product A to increase above $230, because of stiff price competition in this product class. What is the minimum level of estimated sales that would allow you to set this price?

3. (Set all estimated unit sales figures back to their original levels.) If your company increased the profit target to 12%, how would that affect the price to customer?

Exhibit 1. Cost-Plus Pricing Information

Product	A	B	C
Mater. Var. Costs/Unit	$40	$15	$25
Assem. Var. Costs/Unit	10	35	25
Total Var. Costs/Unit	50	50	50
Est. Unit Sales	40000<<	50000<<	35000<<
Fixed Costs	$4,500,000	$2,400,000	$5,300,000
Fixed Costs/Unit	$112.50	$48.00	$151.43
Total Costs/Unit	$162.50	$98.00	$201.43
Profit Target (%)	10%<<	10%	10%
Profit Target ($)	$16.25	$9.80	$20.14
Factory Price	$178.75	$107.80	$221.57
Dealer Markup (25% of Factory Price)	$44.69	$26.95	$55.39
Price to Customer	$223.44	$134.75	$276.96

MACRO COMMANDS PROVIDED:
(Alt)C: To change estimates in spreadsheet as shown in Exhibit 1.
(Alt)P: To print spreadsheet.

File Name: NATIONAL

5.3 NATIONAL ELECTRIC

National Electric was developing a plan for introducing its videodisc player to the market in 1981. The player had been tentatively priced to retail to consumers at $500 with retailers receiving a $200 margin. National had developed an advertising and sales promotion plan on a $22 million budget, and management had estimated that direct fixed production and selling costs would amount to $20 million annually. Variable production costs for 1981 were projected at $100 per unit.

Because the company had already sunk $200 million into the development of the product, top management hoped to obtain a first-year target total contribution to indirect costs and profit of $20 million. (See contribution margin in Exhibit 1.)

Management saw two emerging product forms that might compete for the same home entertainment market needs as the videodisc player. Videocassette recorders (which enabled the customer to record as well as to play prerecorded films and shows) had been priced from $600 to $2000 but, recently, extensive "discounting" had taken place at the retail level with many recorders being offered by as much as $200 off the list price. Additionally, syndicated cable television services such as Home Box Office and Showtime provided cable subscribers with a broader array of movies and other special entertainment offerings at moderately low monthly rates. Finally, two competitors were entering the videodisc market.

Management believed that the market potential for the videodisc player consisted of all households with color television sets (about 80% of households)--a market much broader than the market for cable or videocassette recorders. Videocassette player sales had grown from about 450,000 units in 1979 to 800,000 units in 1980.

The product manager in charge of the videodisc player wondered whether it would be advisable to reduce the suggested retail price to $450 (while preserving the dollar margins earned by retailers).

1. What level of sales is required in the first year if National is to achieve its target total contribution?

2. What level of sales would be needed if National were to lower the suggested retail price to $450, while preserving retailer unit margins?

3. How sensitive are required total sales to changes in per-unit variable costs? To retail prices (assume retailer margins are constant)? To fixed costs of production? Try a few combinations, and discuss your results.

4. (Reset variable costs to original value.) If the price is lowered from $500 to $450, what coefficient of elasticity will be necessary to make up for the difference in unit sales required (from Questions 1 and 2)? (Use the lower part of the worksheet as indicated in Exhibit 1.)

5. Carefully interpret the minimum required elasticity.

6. Based on the factors influencing elasticity, do you think this market is elastic? Explain.

7. Redo Question 4, using different levels of per unit variable costs. (Try $80 and $120.) Discuss the relationship between variable costs, required total sales, and minimum required elasticity. Is minimum required elasticity very sensitive to changes in variable cost?

Exhibit 1. National Electric Worksheet

Retail price:	$500<<
Retailer's margin:	$200
Manuf. price to retailers:	$300
Direct fixed costs of promotion:	$22,000,000
Direct fixed costs of prodn. & sell.:	$20,000,000
Variable production costs:	$100<<
Target total contribution:	$20,000,000

From your calculations above, enter:

Higher price:	$0<<
Required sales level at higher price:	0<<
Lower price:	$0<<
Required sales level at lower price:	0<<
Minimum required coeff. of elasticity:	0

MACRO COMMAND PROVIDED:
(Alt)P: To print main screen.

File Name: EASTSIDE

5.4 EASTSIDE CONSTRUCTION CO.

The Eastside Construction Company is considering bidding for a project valued in the $1 million range. Although a few bids are expected to be tendered, Eastside believes that it can easily underbid all competitors except the Big City Development Company, which is the only other serious bidder. The contract will be awarded to the lowest bidder.

If Eastside sets too low a price, its profit will be low or perhaps even negative. If too high a price is set, then the chances are that Big City will win the contract. Thus, Eastside must determine a bid price that affords them a reasonable chance of winning the contract but is high enough to give them an acceptable profit level. One way a company can assess and compare bid prices is to determine the expected profit from each price, done simply by the following:

Profit if contract is won   x   Probability of winning

So if either profit or probability of winning is too low, the expected profit will be low. The best bid price is one that maximizes expected profit.

Eastside has bid head-to-head with Big City on dozens of projects. Based on this previous bidding history, Eastside has figured out the probability that it will win (i.e., its bid will be lower than that of Big City), given any bid. As shown in Exhibit 1, the bids are expressed in terms of percentage of direct costs. Thus, at a bid of 80% of direct costs, Eastside believes it has a 95% chance of winning--but, of course, would lose money in the process! At a bid of 144% of direct costs, Eastside would make a 44% markup if it won but stands a very poor chance of winning (only 3%).

Direct costs of this project have been assessed by Eastside at $700,000.

1. What is the probability of underbidding Big City with a bid of 80%, 100%, 120%, or 140% of direct costs? Try also a number of other bids in between. Plot the probabilities of winning against bid level.

2. What is the profit that Eastside would obtain if it won the contract at each of the bid prices you tried in Question 1? Plot the profit if the bid is won against bid level.

3. What is the expected profit to Eastside for each of the bid prices you tried in Question 1? (Also try some other bids as well

at this point.) Plot expected profit against bid level.

4. From the point of view of maximizing expected profit, which is the optimum bid?

5. What problems are associated with this method of analysis?

Exhibit 1. Bid Level, Expected Profit at that bid, and Expected Probability of Winning at various bid levels

Estimated direct costs:	$700,000
Bid:	$560,000<< (80% dir. costs)
Prob. of Winning (see below)	95%
Profit (Loss) if Won:	($140,000)
Expected Profit (Loss):	($133,360)

Bid (% of dir. costs)	Probability of Winning
80%	95%
83%	94%
87%	91%
90%	88%
94%	83%
97%	79%
101%	71%
105%	62%
109%	52%
114%	40%
118%	31%
123%	21%
128%	14%
133%	9%
139%	5%
144%	3%

MACRO COMMANDS PROVIDED:
(Alt)C: To change bid.
(Alt)G: To save PrintGraph files (probability of winning vs. bid level; profit if won vs. bid level; expected profit vs. bid level).
(Alt)P: To print screen.

File Name: BUSINESS

5.5 BUSINESS APPLICATIONS, INC.

Business Applications, Inc. is a computer software manufacturer specializing in programs useful to small business managers. They currently produce two software packages, A and B. Package A is the more complex and detailed, and it sells to retailers for $399. Package B, a trimmed-down version with less capability and documentation, sells for $169. Other costs are provided in Exhibit 1.

Last year, Business Applications sold 6,281 copies of Package A and 40,522 copies of Package B. Exhibit 1 shows that Business Applications gets a far bigger contribution margin per unit from Package A and is considering a price cut to stimulate sales of this product. Of course, they realize that A and B are substitutes, so to determine the net impact on company profit, Business Applications must look at the cross effects and product cannibalization rates.

Based on familiarity with similar products, company management estimates that the sales level of Package A varies with price as follows:

$$S_A = 1{,}000{,}000 \times P_A^{-2}$$

They believe that, if Package A's price is lowered, the cannibalization rate will be 15%. That is, 15% of the increase in Package A's sales will come from customers who otherwise would have bought Package B.

1. Assuming a 15% cannibalization rate, what price should Business Applications set for Package A in order to maximize total company profit? How many more units of Package A would be sold with this new pricing policy? How many units of Package B would be cannibalized?

2. Suppose Package A's variable cost per unit is expected to increase by 10% next year. Does this change the profit-maximizing price?

3. (Reset variable cost of Package A to original level.) Much of the analysis hinges on the projection of a 15% cannibalization rate. Show how sensitive optimum Package A price and company profit are to changes in the cannibalization rate. (Try a couple of rates above, and a couple below, 15%).

Exhibit 1. Business Applications Inc. Contribution Analysis

	Package A	Package B	Co. Totals
	==========	==========	==========
Cannib. Rate		15%<<	
Manuf. Price	$399<<	$169	
Quant.Sold (000s)	6281	40522	46803
Var. Costs	$160<<	$125	
Contr.Mgn./Unit	$239	$44	
V.C.M.	$1,501,247	$1,782,966	
Fixed Costs	$800,000	$500,000	
C.I.C.P.	$701,247	$1,282,966	$1,984,212
Indir. F.C.			$1,250,000
Co. Profit			$734,212

MACRO COMMANDS PROVIDED:
(Alt)C: To change estimates as indicated in Exhibit 1.
(Alt)P: To print screen.

PART 6: ADVERTISING PROGRAMS

6.1 General Brands (GENERAL)
6.2 Sunscreen, Inc. (SUNSCR)
6.3 Vidale-Wolfe Model Exercise (VIDALE)
6.4 Whittaker Products, Inc. (WHITT)
6.5 Media Planning Exercise (MEDIAE)

File Name: GENERAL

6.1 GENERAL BRANDS

General Brands manufactures a wide line of specialty food products, including several new lines of frozen dinner entrees. Among the new dinner entrees was the Monterrey line of frozen Mexican foods, introduced in 1983. Although the product had been received positively by consumers, market share had slipped in recent years. However, the company had managed to maintain a relatively stable sales volume while reducing advertising expenditures per case.

Near the end of 1987, the product manager for the Monterrey line was contemplating how much to spend on advertising in 1988. Recent research had revealed that the Monterrey line was widely preferred on taste tests to its two major competitors, and price and distribution were comparable to the competition. However, only 61% of consumers were aware of the Monterrey brand, compared to 71% and 73% for competing brands. On a per case basis, retailers priced the product at $10 and took a $2 margin. Manufacturers' variable costs were estimated at $3.20 per case, and direct fixed costs for selling and production were $2.2 million. The advertising budget for fiscal 1987 (10/86-9/87) was $1,282,000 (additional data in Exhibit 1).

Both major competitors had increased their market shares in 1987. Shares increased to 42% for Gomez brand and 30% for the Enrique brand. Additionally, both competing firms were bringing a number of other specialty foods to the market in 1987. Analysis of competitors' media usage indicated that all three firms were attaining comparable levels of frequency of exposure but that Monterrey trailed in gross rating points by a substantial amount. After analyzing alternative media schedules, the advertising agency used for the Monterrey line determined that additional expenditures of $1 million would be needed to match competitors' current levels of reach without reducing frequency levels. (A contribution margin analysis for Monterrey is provided in Exhibit 2.)

1. For each quarter, industry sales, advertising to sales ratio, competitive advertising, and Monterrey advertising share are provided in the accompanying spreadsheet. Plot Monterrey sales, Monterrey advertising expenditure, Monterrey market share, industry sales, and Monterrey advertising share to illustrate how these have changed through time.

2. What can you learn about competitive advertising behavior and about sales response to advertising in this industry by looking at the patterns you plotted for Question 1?

3. Assess current contribution to indirect costs and profit, and determine required level of sales in 1988 to maintain C.I.C.P. if the $1 million advertising increase is implemented. Express sales requirement in dollars and in units.

4. What market share is required for General Brands to meet their required 1988 sales level, assuming no industry sales growth? What market share would be required if there is a 10% growth in industry sales in 1988?

5. Present the basic arguments you would use in recommending the $1 million increase in your advertising budget. Include a discussion of the advertising objectives you would establish, and indicate any other ways in which you would change the pattern of advertising expenditures.

MACRO COMMANDS PROVIDED:
(Alt)G: To save PrintGraph files (company share, company advertising, company market share, industry sales, and company advertising share vs. time).
(Alt)C: To change estimates (industry sales growth rate and company case sales projections).
(Alt)P: To print the contribution analysis.

Exhibit 1. Company and Industry Historical Data

Months	Monterrey Case Sales (1000's)	Monterrey Advert. ($1000's)	Monterrey Market Share	Tot. Indust. Advertising ($1000's)
1984 Jul-Sep	192	585	28	2017
Oct-Dec	196	507	26	2192
1985 Jan-Mar	200	468	24	2272
Apr-Jun	204	505	25	2104
Jul-Sep	198	480	24	2086
Oct-Dec	196	390	24	2052
1986 Jan-Mar	202	355	22	2088
Apr-Jun	198	330	22	2062
Jul-Sep	200	330	22	2050
Oct-Dec	204	360	23	1894
1987 Jan-Mar	214	312	21	1950
Apr-Jun	200	298	21	2048
Jul-Sep	214	312	21	1960
Oct-Dec	-	320	-	-

Exhibit 2. Monterrey Contribution Analysis

	10/86-9/87	10/87-9/88
Rate of Ind. Sales Growth		0.00%<<
Monterrey Case Sales	832000	832000 <<
Industry Case Sales	3877440	3877440
Monterrey's Mkt. Share	21.46%	21.46%
Retail Sales at $10/case	$8,320,000	$8,320,000
- Ret. Mgns. $2/case	1,664,000	1,664,000
- Var. Cost $3.20/case	2,662,400	2,662,400
Var. Contrib. Mgn.	3,993,600	3,993,600
Dir. Fixed Costs		
- Prodn. and Sales	2,200,000	2,200,000
- Advertising	1,282,000	2,282,000
Total Contribution	$511,600	($488,400)

File Name: SUNSCR

6.2 SUNSCREEN, INC.

Ron Dyce had been employed as a sales representative for Colgate Palmolive for several years in the Daytona Beach area. In his spare time, he and a former college classmate had developed a line of sunscreen and suntanning products with the assistance of a local chemistry teacher. They had sold these under the brand names of Sunseeker and Sunaway for the past three years.

They felt that reception to these products had been good, and they had reached the point where they wanted to expand their sales. They were considering increasing the advertising budget for 1984. In reviewing their annual performance for 1983, they concluded that past sales and advertising expenditures indicated diminishing returns from advertising. They estimated that sales fluctuated proportionately to $[A(t)/A(t-1)]^{0.68}$, where $A(t)$ was the advertising budget for the period in which sales were forecasted and $A(t-1)$ was the previous period's advertising budget. They also felt that if advertising was kept at the same amount, sales in 1984 would remain unchanged from 1983. Basic costs and sales data for the two products for the year 1983 were as given in Exhibit 1.

1. With a limit of $7,000 to spend on advertising for the two products in 1984, they wondered how they should allocate their budget between the two products to maximize their profit. Help them make this allocation decision.

2. Would your advertising allocation change if cost of sales of each product increased by $0.05 a unit? If they decreased by $0.05 a unit? Should you be concerned about possible sales cost changes of this magnitude when allocating advertising budget?

Exhibit 1. Contribution Analysis by Product Line

	Sunseeker	Sunaway
Sales per year (bottles)	14000	20000
Unit price	$0.80	$0.96
Cost of sales	0.50<<	0.70<<
Selling and Administrative Costs (excluding advertising)	0.14	0.10
Sales Revenue	11,200	19,200
Variable Contribution Margin	2,240	3,200
Advertising in Daytona Beach area in 1983	1,000	2,000
Total Contribution	1,240	1,200

1984 Advertising Budgets:
  Sunseeker: 4,500<<
  Sunaway: 2,500<<
Total: 7,000

MACRO COMMAND PROVIDED:
(Alt)P: To print main screen.

<u>Note</u>: This problem is based on the Sunscreen case in Guiltinan and Paul's second edition manual.

File Name: VIDALE

6.3 VIDALE-WOLFE MODEL EXERCISE

There are a number of marketing models that relate advertising levels to sales volumes. One of these (by Vidale and Wolfe) uses a factor in exponential form to determine the effect advertising spending has on sales volumes. We shall examine how this model works in this problem.

One of the advantages of this model is that it only requires the user to estimate a few constants. Two of these are the sales-response constant and the sales-decay constant. Sales-response constant is estimated as the sales generated per dollar of advertising when sales level equals zero; that is, if this constant is 10, then $10 of additional sales would be generated if the company spends $1 in advertising. The sales-decay constant is the proportion of sales lost per unit of time when advertising equals zero. So, if this constant is 0.2, and this month's sales were 1000 units, then sales would fall to 800 units if advertising was stopped.

The model itself is complicated; if you want to see what it looks like, it appears in the accompanying LOTUS spreadsheet. What is important for the purposes of this problem is that, if you give the sales-response and sales-decay constants, total market volume, and current sales level, the program will give you projected sales for any monthly advertising level. (For this problem, we assume you spend the same amount on advertising every month. A more complex version of the program would allow you to vary the monthly advertising budget also, but we won't worry about that for now.) If you have contribution margin per unit and fixed costs as well as projected sales, you can project profits. The program gives you projected monthly profits and also discounted profits.

The program assumes that monthly fixed costs are your advertising expenditures plus $50,000 of other fixed costs and that the monthly discount rate is 0.003%, as shown in Exhibit 1.

1. Find the monthly advertising budget that maximizes cumulative discounted profit. What is the projected cumulative sales level? Plot the pattern of sales and profits through time for this advertising level.

2. Try each of the following situations separately (resetting to original levels before continuing). How does each manipulation affect the profit-maximizing advertising budget and the projected cumulative sales level?
   a. Sales-response constant decreases to 6.
   b. Sales-decay constant increases to 0.2.
   c. P.V.C.M. decreases to 25%.
In each case, explain the observed sales and profit changes.

Exhibit 1. Parameters for Vidale-Wolfe model

Total market volume (units):	1650000
Sales-response constant:	8<<
Sales-decay constant:	0.1<<
Current sales level:	220000
Your advertising budget per month:	80000<<
P.V.C.M.:	35%<<
Projected Cumulative Sales:	$14,010,426
Projected Cumulative Discounted Profit:	$3,272,310

MACRO COMMANDS PROVIDED:
(Alt)C: To change parameters (market volume, sales-response and sales-decay constants, sales level, advertising budget, P.V.C.M.).
(Alt)G: To save PrintGraph file (sales and profits vs. time).
(Alt)P: To print screen.

File Name: WHITT

6.4 WHITTAKER PRODUCTS INC.

Whittaker Products manufactures and distributes items of stationery over a three-state region. Among their product line is a high-quality fine line marker pen favored by artists, engineers, and students which Whittaker currently sells to retailers at $15.00 for a carton of ten. The company incurs variable costs of production of $0.90 per marker, and variable costs of sales amount to $0.05 per marker. Fixed costs incurred during 1984 were as follows: Fixed cost of production, $15,000; fixed cost of advertising, $8,100. Currently the company produces and sells 50,000 markers annually.

Sales of this marker are responsive to changes in Whittaker's advertising and pricing policies, and price setting for this product must take into account the advertising policy chosen.

The company feels that, in the absence of competitive retaliation, the sales of the marker can be expressed as follows:

$$S = 30{,}000 \times A^{0.2} \times P^{-2},$$

where S = sales volume (in units),
A = advertising level,
and P = price.

Retailers receive a fixed margin on the product; hence, an increase in price to manufacturers is passed on to the consumer as an increase in retail price. Exhibit 1 contains further cost information you will require.

1. To what level would advertising have to be increased for the company to stimulate the sale of 90,000 units annually, assuming price to manufacturer remains unchanged and the equation relating sales to advertising is reasonably accurate?

2. Assume the company can sell all it produces. What would be the saving in average total unit production cost (economy of scale) if production volume increased to 90,000 units annually (assuming fixed costs of production remain unchanged)?

3. What would the total contribution to the company be, if they increased their production volume to 90,000 units per year <u>and</u> raised their advertising level to the amount you recommended in Question 2? Based on this observed change in total contribution, would you recommend that the firm increase production volume?

4. Suppose that the company cannot afford to increase its advertising budget beyond $11,000 per year due to internal budget constraints. To what level would the company have to lower its price to retailers of its box of 10 units, in order to stimulate sales of the desired 90,000 units?

5. How would the advertising budget constraint change the total contribution you found in Question 3? Would you change your recommendation to the company?

6. Keep the advertising budget at $11,000. What price level maximizes total contribution margin? Would this change your recommendation? Why or why not?

Exhibit 1. Whittaker Products Contribution Analysis

Advertising	$8,100<<
Price (per 10 units)	$15.00<<
Price per unit	$1.50
Sales volume	80656
Sales revenue	$120,984
Var. cost of prodn. per unit	$0.90
Total var. cost of prodn.	$72,590
Var. cost of sales	$4,033
Total variable costs	$76,623
Var. Contrib. Margin	$44,361
Fixed costs of prodn.	$15,000
Total costs of prodn.	$87,590
Avg. unit cost of prodn.	$1.09
Total fixed costs (prodn. + adv.)	$23,100
Total contrib. margin	$21,261

MACRO COMMAND PROVIDED:
(Alt)P: To print screen.

File Name: MEDIAE

6.5 MEDIA PLANNING EXERCISE

Your company has developed a new line of executive women's wear called "First Class." The line is designed to be elegant and feminine, yet functional and appropriate for the boardroom. The target market for the product is working women, aged 25-49, living in your region of the country. The market is estimated to consist of 5 million prospects. You now are in charge of developing an advertising campaign for the "First Class" line. One of your major tasks is to choose a media strategy.

You have chosen magazines (with an edition for your region of the country) as the best media category for women's business apparel. You have identified four magazines as being the most appropriate vehicles for the advertising campaign. They are as follows:

* U.S. Woman (working woman audience)
* Business and Finance (financial advice and information)
* Parachute (career and job-hunting advice)
* American Week (newsmagazine)

Each of these magazines is published once a month. You have obtained the page costs and readerships for each:

* U.S. Woman: page cost = $12,000; readership = 1,750,000
* Business and Finance: $15,000; 2,929,000
* Parachute: $9,000; 2,050,000
* American Week: $21,000; 6,000,000.

You have also determined from demographic analysis that 90% of U.S. Woman readers are prospects (in your target market); the comparable figures for Business and Finance, Parachute, and American Week are 62.5%, 50%, and 40%.

You have obtained data on audience duplication. For each pair of magazines, you know how many prospects read both (and therefore are exposed to your ad twice per month). These figures are given in the computer spreadsheet.

1. Make a recommendation on a media plan. Should your company choose two, three, or all four magazines? Which combination would you recommend? Back up your recommendation with a clear consideration of reach, total cost, and cost per thousand.

2. Supposing a fifth magazine, Modern Life, became available as an alternate choice. The page cost to advertise in Modern Life is $25,000. It has a readership of 5 million, of which 23% are prospects. You have the following audience duplication data:

Duplication between: Size of duplicated audience:
    U.S. Woman & Modern Life   300,000
    Bus. and Fin. & Modern Life   300,000
    Parachute & Modern Life   200,000
    Amer. Week & Modern Life   325,000

How does the presence of this fifth magazine change your recommendation in Question 1? Would you recommend adding Modern Life to your list of media vehicles? (Do this problem by hand.)

MACRO COMMANDS PROVIDED:
(Alt)P,Q,R,S: To print various portions of the spreadsheet.

ESTIMATING REACH FOR MAGAZINE INSERTIONS

We can estimate the reach for any combination of two or more magazines using a simple formula calculated by Agostini in 1961:

$C = A / [K(D/A) + 1]$, where
C = total reach,
K = 1.125 (a constant),
A = total number of prospects in magazine's audience,
D = total of all pairwise duplicated audiences (this means we must take each possible pair of magazines).

For example, if you wanted to estimate the reach you would get by advertising in Magazines X, Y, and Z, you would calculate A and D as:

A = X's total audience + Y's total audience + Z's total audience;

D = all prospects covered by both X and Y + all prospects covered by both Y and Z + all prospects covered by both X and Z.

Calculating A and D in this way and substituting into the above equation gives you an estimate of overall reach (total number of prospects exposed at least once) that is quite accurate.

PART 7: SALES PROMOTION PROGRAMS

7.1 Gasoline Promotion Model (GASOLINE)
7.2 Harris Company (HARRIS)
7.3 Treasure Isle Seafood Company (TREASURE)
7.4 Chef Alphonse (ALPHONSE)
7.5 Burger Master (BURGER)

File Name: GASOLINE

7.1 GASOLINE PROMOTION MODEL

You have undoubtedly seen contests in which a customer gets a game form from a participating retailer. The game may be a sweepstakes where winners are selected at random every month. These games are used offensively by retailers like gasoline companies to draw customers away from competitive brands and also defensively to prevent the loss of customers to competitive brands.

Rao and Lilien (1972) developed a model that used an aggregate approach to determine the incremental sales gain from running a gasoline promotional game. They looked at the following three factors:

a. Promotion potential: this is related to the fraction of individuals who are not current purchasers of the promoting brand. If the market share of the promoting brand is m, then the maximum proportion of gasoline buyers that can be switched is (1-m). This is an indication of purchase potential, P. So we have

$$P = (1 - m).$$

b. Promotion reach: the more outlets the brand has in a given area, the easier it is for a customer to participate. This is related to m, the brand's market share, but not linearly. If R is reach,

$$R = m^a,$$

where a is a number less than one.

c. Promotion strength: the more interesting a promotion is to the customer, the more likely he or she will participate in it and take advantage of the possibility of winning. We will call promotion strength S.

The probability that a randomly chosen customer will respond to the promotion is

$$P \times R \times S.$$

Given all this, the gasoline company can determine the expected gain per customer responding to promotion, V*, as

$$V^* = P \times R \times S \times g,$$

where g is the average quantity purchased by each customer during the promotional period.

If there are C customers in the market, then the incremental sales gain obtained by the promoting brand is V, where

$$V = P \times R \times S \times G,$$

where $G = g \times C$.

Since we have forms for P and R above, we can substitute to get the following:

$$V = (1 - m)(m^a)(S)(G).$$

We are considering a promotion for a product with a variable contribution margin of $4.50. Average quantity purchased per customer during the promotion is 50 units, and fixed cost of the promotion is estimated at $160,000. Other parameters and estimates are as given in Exhibit 1.

1. Estimate the incremental sales gain and the net profit impact for a number of market shares from 0 to 100%, given S, G, and a. How do incremental sales gain and net profit impact behave? (Show graphs of sales gain and profit impact versus market share.)

2. At what market share are sales gain and net profit impact maximized?

3. How sensitive is your optimal market share to decreases in promotional strength index and average quantity purchased during promotion? Try each of the following separately, resetting to original values before continuing:
   a. A promotion strength index of 0.9.
   b. An average quantity purchased per customer during promotion of 40 units.
Plot graphs that show these effects, and explain your findings.

4. (Reset promotional strength index and average quantity purchased to original values.) What is the minimum market share that would make this promotion worthwhile? (That is, at what market share would the net profit impact of this promotion be zero?) How can we interpret this market share?

5. Should large-share gas companies use this kind of promotion? Medium-share? Small-share? Why or why not? What do you think accounts for these differences?

Exhibit 1. Parameters and Estimates for Gasoline Promotion Model

Company's market share:	m:	15%<<
Promotion strength index:	S:	1<<
Avg. quantity purchased per customer during promotion (units):	g:	50<<
Number of customers in market:	C:	20000
Promotion potential:	P:	0.85
Promotion reach:	R:	0.387
Incremental sales gain to promoting brand (units):	V:	329204
Var. Contr. Margin per Unit:		$4.50
Increase in Contribution due to Promotion:		$1,481,416
Fixed Cost of Promotion:		$1,168,000
Net Profit Impact of Promotion:		$313,416

MACRO COMMANDS PROVIDED:
(Alt)G: To graph sales gain and profit impact against market share.
(Alt)C: To change market share, promotional strength index, or quantity purchased during promotion.
(Alt)P: To print screen.

File Name: HARRIS

7.2 HARRIS COMPANY

The Harris Company is a food processing company with sales throughout the continental United States. Frozen foods make up a large share of their total sales volume. Harris sells a brand of frozen orange juice that normally retails at $2.19 per can. The product is sold to retailers at $1.99 per can, allowing them to make a $0.20 margin on each can sold. Variable costs are estimated at $0.95 per can. In a typical month, 8 million units are sold nationwide.

Because of heavy promotional expenditures by competitors, Harris is concerned about losing market share. In order to protect itself, Harris management is thinking of running price specials on their brand of orange juice. The price special would run for one month. Management figured that the sales level during the promotional period would be somewhat higher than for normal months. Some of this sales increase would be due to current customers stocking up, and some would come from customers who usually don't buy the Harris brand. It was felt that some of these latter customers would begin to buy Harris on a more regular basis after the promotion, since the product was comparable in flavor, texture and vitamin content to all other leading brands.

The product manager was trying to decide which of three possible sales promotions to recommend. There were a few factors involved in the decision. First, the larger the retail price reduction, the greater the increase in sales during the promotional period would be. However, if the reduction was substantial, it is possible that the retailer's margin would be reduced, and fewer retailers would be interested in going along with the price reduction. (They would continue to sell the Harris brand at the regular price.) This could be critical, since the lower the level of dealer participation, the lower the number of potential customers reached by the promotion.

The promotions under consideration were as follows:

a. Reduce retail price by $0.15; maintain dealer's margin at $0.20. Based on experiences with similar products, the product manager felt that 90% of retailers would participate in this promotion. Total brand sales would be forecasted to increase by 5% in markets reached by the promotion (no effect on sales in markets not reached by the promotion).

b. Reduce retail price by $0.25; reduce dealer's margin by $0.05. Only 65% of retailers would participate in this promotion. The

$0.25 price reduction would cause sales in the affected markets to increase by 15%.

c. Reduce retail price by $0.30; reduce dealer's margin by $0.05, 65% of retailers would participate; sales in the affected markets would increase by 20%.

1. What is the current variable contribution? What would the variable contribution be under each of the sales promotions?

2. For sales promotion a, how many more units of orange juice would have to be sold <u>after</u> the promotion is over in order to maintain the current level of C.I.C.P.? How would this be affected if your estimates of dealer participation were off? (Try a few possibilities here.) Answer the same question for sales promotions b and c.

3. For each of the three alternatives, how great would the sales increase during the promotion have to be in order for total contribution during the promotional period to be maintained?

4. What factors aside from dollar amounts should you also consider?

5. Consider another promotion where a full $0.50 is taken off the retail price. As a result of past experiences, the product manager believes that this would cause a sizeable increase in sales at stores running the promotion during the promotional month. Selling price to retailers is low enough for them to maintain their current per-unit margin. (That is, you absorb the margin lost due to the price reduction.) Estimated rate (percentage) of dealer participation will be 90%. How great would the sales increase during the promotion period have to be in order to maintain total contribution? How is your answer affected if retailers' margins were reduced by $0.10 and dealer participation decreased to 50%? Would you recommend that Harris use either of these price promotions? Why or why not?

Exhibit 1. Spreadsheet for Assessing Effect of Promotions

Level of dealer participation
   (% of market reached by promotion):   0%<<
Price discount per unit: $0<<
Reduction in retail margin per unit: $0<<
Forecasted increase in sales during promotion: 0%<<

MACRO COMMANDS PROVIDED:
(Alt)C: To change parameters in Exhibit 1.
(Alt)P: To print main screen.

File Name: TREASURE

7.3 TREASURE ISLE SEAFOOD COMPANY

Treasure Isle Seafood Company is introducing a new stuffed flounder food item to its frozen seafood product line. The new 24-ounce package (four 6-ounce stuffed flounder per consumer package) will retail at $7.98 each. The retailer pays $5.50 each ($55.00 per case; ten consumer packages per case). The Treasure Isle comptroller estimates the production variable cost per case of stuffed flounder to be $33.50.

Treasure Isle has asked you, the product manager, to test the market acceptance of the new item in a southwest city. You have chosen Houston and have estimated the following product introduction costs for a one-month promotional event.

a. one-month coupon sales promotion: $1.00 per package savings to consumers. Retailers are given $1.00 credit on each unit purchased once they have tendered the redeemed coupon. The objective of the coupon promotion is to attract new users.

b. $5,000 cooperative advertising support to participating retailers.

c. $15,000 television media expense to make customers aware of the new product introduction.

d. $2,500 for the design and production of in-store displays to be used to introduce the new item at the frozen seafood section of the food store.

e. $1,500 for local advertisements, mailers, in-store promotional aids sent to food chain buyers and merchandisers to create retailer awareness, interest, and participation in the new product introduction.

f. $0.07 per coupon redemption cost awarded to retailers for handling consumer coupon redemptions.

Your experience in previous similar coupon promotions for new seafood products leads you to believe retailers in the Houston area will sell about 1,200 cases of the stuffed flounder during the one-month promotion. An additional 550 cases will be sold the next month after the introductory event and can be attributed to repeat purchases by the new users. You believe, also, that 70% of the promotion-month sales will come from coupon redemptions.

1. Determine the P.V.C.M. for products purchased with coupons during the one-month coupon promotion event.

2. Determine the C.I.C.P. that would be expected if the sales estimates are correct. Is the contribution margin generated by the product sufficient to liquidate the direct fixed cost of introducing the new product into the Houston market?

3. How sensitive is the C.I.C.P. you determined in Question 2 to variations in estimates of total sales (during and after promotion)? How sensitive is C.I.C.P. to variations in the proportion of sales due to coupon promotions? What conclusions can you draw from this analysis? (See Exhibit 1.)

4. (Set all variables back to original estimates.) Assume that Treasure Isle currently sells a 16-ounce package of flounder fillets (retail price: $4.98). Treasure Isle price to retailers is $3.38, and variable production cost is $2.03. Fifteen percent of total stuffed flounder sales come from displaced fillet sales. What impact do the displaced sales of fillets have on the contribution margin toward liquidating the cost of promotion? (See Exhibit 2.)

5. How sensitive is your answer in Question 4 to variations in the estimated displacement rate (Exhibit 2)? What conclusions can you draw?

Exhibit 1. Treasure Isle Contribution Analysis

Variable contribution during promotional month:

	Coupon	Noncoupon	Total
Percent of total sales:	70%<<	30%	
Sales (Cases):	840	360	1200<<
VCM per case:	$10.80	$21.50	
Var. Contrib. for month:	9072	7740	16812

Variable contribution due to repeat purchases after promo month:

Sales (Cases):		0<<	
VCM per case:		$21.50	
Var. Contrib. for month:		$0	$0
Total var. contr. for promo. and repeat sales:			$16812
- Direct fixed cost of product introduction:			$24000
Net total contr. to indirect costs and profits:			($7188)

Exhibit 2. Treasure Isle Displaced Sales Analysis

Manuf. selling price per unit of fillets:	$3.38
Var. prodn. cost per unit:	$2.03
Var. Contr. Mgn. per unit:	$1.35
Percent of stuffed flounder sales coming from displaced fillet sales:	15%<<
Total stuffed flounder sales (cases):	1200
Total stuffed flounder sales (units):	12000
Displaced fillet sales (units):	1800
VCM lost due to displaced fillet sales:	$2430

MACRO COMMANDS PROVIDED:
(Alt)C: To change values as indicated in Exhibits 1 and 2.
(Alt)P: To print contribution analysis spreadsheet.
(Alt)Q: To print displaced sales analysis spreadsheet.

Note: This problem was developed and written by Prof. Samuel M. Gillespie of Texas A & M University.

File Name: ALPHONSE

7.4 CHEF ALPHONSE

Al Smith is marketing manager of a restaurant chain, Chef Alphonse, which serves the Southwest portion of the United States. Sales per restaurant total $12,000 per week. In the three-state region (California, Nevada, and Arizona) served by Chef Alphonse outlets, the restaurant has a market share of about 15%. Mr. Smith knows that this represents a decrease of a few market share points as compared to last year. The chief competitors, various other restaurant chains, have been successful in drawing away market share through the use of contests, sweepstakes, and clever advertising. Mr. Smith thinks that a new coupon promotion for Chef Alphonse might help to stop this share erosion.

Mr. Smith is considering a one-week coupon offer for a free barbecued chicken. Half-page ads would be taken out in newspapers serving a market area containing twenty Chef Alphonse restaurants. Each ad would contain one clip-out coupon. Total cost of printing and advertising space in the papers would be $32,000, and a total of 1,200,000 coupons would be distributed (since this is the total circulation of all newspapers involved).

Regular price of a barbecued chicken (prepared with the Chef's secret recipe of 2,494 herbs and spices) is $1.80. All products sold at Chef Alphonse are priced such that variable costs are 50% of selling price (so variable contribution margin must also be 50%). Based on previous promotional campaigns, Mr. Smith expects redemption rates of the coupons to be 4%, and 30% of the redeemers to be regular customers. Incidentally, Mr. Smith knows that the average customer purchase per visit to a Chef Alphonse outlet is approximately $2.80.

1. If Mr. Smith's market response estimates are correct, what increase in noncoupon sales volume must Chef Alphonse achieve in order to offset the direct cost and the loss in various contribution associated with this program? (Do this problem by hand.) Where might these additional sales come from?

2. From your spreadsheet analysis, what is the projected change in total contribution and the number of visits by converts after the promotion required to offset this reduced contribution? How would this change if the cost of the promotion were to increase by 10%?

3. (Set cost of promotion back to original level.) Mr. Smith is wondering what would happen if the value of the coupon were reduced from $1.80. He believes that, if the value were reduced, the response rate would decline and the displacement rate would

increase. He assumes that, during the coupon period, displaced buyers will still purchase an additional $1.00 in products. (Recall that the price of a chicken is $1.80, but the average customer purchase per visit is $2.80; about $1.00 on average is spent on coffee plus dessert.) Mr. Smith thinks that new buyers will also purchase an additional $1.00 per visit. New buyers who return to the restaurant following the coupon period are, however, expected to average $2.80 per visit in purchases. Analyze and evaluate Mr. Smith's assumptions regarding the relationship between coupon value and redemption rate and between coupon value and displacement rate. (To do this, try several levels for coupon value, and note how redemption rate and displacement rate are affected.)

4. Examine the effects of changes in coupon value on:
   a. number of coupons redeemed by new buyers
   b. number of coupons redeemed by displaced buyers
   c. change in total contribution
   d. average number of visits required per convert to offset the reduction in total contribution.
(Do each of these separately.) Explain all observations clearly.

5. (Set coupon value back to original level.) Mr. Smith's analysis depends greatly on his assumptions about drag-along sales. He is not really too sure of that estimate of $1.00 per new customer. How are your results (change in total contribution and number of visits required by converts) affected if a lower drag-along rate were attained? (Try $0.80 and $0.90.) Does the rate of drag-along sales make a big difference in your results? Explain your observations clearly.

6. Would you recommend that Chef Alphonse proceed with this program? Why or why not? (Be sure to consider what sales promotion objective is appropriate in framing your answer.)

Exhibit 1. Analysis of Net Impact of Coupon Promotion

Coupons distributed:	1200000
Coupon value:	$1.80<<
Redemption rate:	4%
Displacement rate:	30%
Average sales per visit:	$2.80
Dragalong sales per new customer during sales promotion:	$1.00<<
Average sales per visit for converts:	$2.80
Cost of coupon promotion:	$32,000<<
PVCM:	$0.50

MACRO COMMANDS PROVIDED:
(Alt)C: To change coupon value, drag-along sales to new customers, and cost of promotion.
(Alt)P: To print main screen.

NOTE TO CHEF ALPHONSE CASE

To assist you in solving this case, the main spreadsheet provides the following information:

a. The net impact (reduction) in contribution resulting from the proposed sales promotion.

b. The increase in post-promotion sales to converts (that is, customers who are initially attracted by the promotion but come back after the promotion and buy at the regular price) required to offset the reduction in contribution caused by the promotion.

c. The required number of visits by converts after the promotion to offset the reduction in contribution, assuming a sales level per visit as given in the spreadsheet.

d. The average number of visits required per convert in order to offset the reduction in total contribution.

These figures give you some indication of how expensive the sales promotion will actually be to the company. If the sales promotion initially loses, say, $30,000, but you realistically think you can more than offset that within a month after the promotion due to increased sales, then the promotion doesn't look too unattractive. If it would take you three years to offset the loss in contribution, you may think differently about it.

File Name: BURGER

7.5 BURGER MASTER

Burger Master is a fast-food chain that serves a four-state area in the Midwest. As 1984 drew to a close, it was apparent that Burger Master sales would just barely exceed those of the previous year, averaging $10,000 per week per store. Although precise industry sales data were not available, managers at Burger Master believed that their market share was between 15% and 20% for the total four-state region. However, these managers were confident that the company's share had eroded in the past year, partly because of the success that major competitors had been having with contests, games, and extensive advertising. This prompted Burger Master's director of marketing to consider some new sales promotions.

One promotion under consideration was a one-week coupon offer for a free hamburger and cola. The coupons were to be printed within quarter-page newspaper ads in a market area containing twenty Burger Master outlets. Based on newspaper circulation estimates, about 1 million coupons would be distributed at a total cost (for printing and advertising space) of $20,000. Burger Master's total price for a hamburger and cola was $1.20. All of Burger Master's products were priced so that both the variable cost of the food and the variable contribution margin were 50% of the selling price. Redemption rates were expected to be 3%, with 25% of redeemers expected to be regular customers. The director of marketing also noted that the average customer purchase was approximately $2.20 per visit.

1. If the marketing director's market response estimates are correct, what increase in noncoupon sales volume must Burger Master achieve in order to offset the direct cost and the loss in various contribution associated with this program? (Do this problem by hand.) Where might these additional sales come from?

2. Now the marketing director is wondering what would happen if the value of the coupon were reduced. He believes that, if the value were reduced, the response rate would decline and the displacement rate would increase. He assumes that, during the coupon period, displaced buyers will still purchase an additional $1.00 in products. (Recall that the price of a hamburger and cola is $1.20, but the average customer purchase per visit is $2.20; about $1.00 on average is spent on other purchases.) He thinks that new buyers will only purchase an additional $0.50 per visit, but he is not too sure of this estimate. New buyers who return to the restaurant following the coupon period are, however, expected to average $2.20 per visit in purchases. Assess the implications

of the manager's assumptions. In particular, analyze and evaluate the assumptions regarding the relationship between coupon value and redemption rate and between coupon value and displacement rate. (To do this, try several values for coupon value, and note how redemption rate and displacement rate are affected.)

3. Examine the effects of changes in coupon value on:
   a. number of coupons redeemed by new buyers
   b. number of coupons redeemed by displaced buyers
   c. change in total contribution
   d. average number of visits required from converts to offset the reduction in total contribution.

(Do each of these separately, resetting to original value before continuing.) Explain all your observations clearly.

4. (Set coupon value back to original level.) Compare the effects of such changes for several lower and higher levels of drag-along sales per new customer during the promotion period. Does the rate of drag-along sales make a big difference in your results?

5. Assess the likelihood that Burger Master will obtain the level of required conversions at each coupon value level. Would you recommend that Burger Master proceed with this program? Why or why not? (Be sure to consider what sales promotion objective is appropriate in framing your answer.)

Exhibit 1. Analysis of Net Impact of Coupon Promotion

Coupons distributed:	1000000
Coupon value:	$1.20<<
Redemption rate:	3%
Displacement Rate:	25%
Average sales per visit for regular and displaced customers:	$2.20
Dragalong sales per new customer during promotion:	$0.50<<
Average sales per visit for converts:	$2.20
Cost of coupon promotion:	$20,000
PVCM:	50%

MACRO COMMANDS PROVIDED:
(Alt)C: To change coupon value and drag-along sales per new customer.
(Alt)P: To print main screen.

NOTE TO BURGER MASTER CASE

To assist you in solving this case, the main spreadsheet provides the following information:

a. The net impact (reduction) in contribution resulting from the proposed sales promotion.

b. The increase in post-promotion sales to converts (that is, customers who are initially attracted by the promotion but come back after the promotion and buy at the regular price) required to offset the reduction in contribution caused by the promotion.

c. The required number of visits by converts after the promotion to offset the reduction in contribution, assuming a sales level per visit as given in the spreadsheet.

d. The average number of visits required per convert in order to offset the reduction in total contribution.

These figures give you some indication of how expensive the sales promotion will actually be to the company. If the sales promotion initially loses, say, $30,000, but you realistically think you can more than offset that within a month after the promotion due to increased sales, then the promotion doesn't look too unattractive. If it would take you three years to offset the loss in contribution, you may think differently about it.

Note: This problem is based on the Burger Master case in Guiltinan and Paul's second edition, Chapter 10.

PART 8: SALES AND DISTRIBUTION PROGRAMS

    8.1   Handel, Inc. (HANDEL)
    8.2   Colbert Company (COLBERT)
    8.3   Litebar, Inc. (LITEBAR)
    8.4   Easterly Floor Coverings (EASTERLY)
    8.5   Sales Force Call Planning Exercise (SFCALL)

File Name: HANDEL

8.1 HANDEL, INC.

Handel produced and marketed a line of automated machinery and had sales of $240,000,000 in 1989. Because of general economic conditions, industry sales for 1990 were not expected to grow substantially. At the same time, competition on price and credit terms was expected to stiffen sharply.

Handel had maintained a policy of allowing customers 30 days to pay invoices on shipments of new equipment. Company officials estimated that variable costs for labor, materials, and sales force commissions were 40% of sales. Additionally, the cost of carrying accounts receivable was estimated to be 20% of the average outstanding accounts receivable.

For 1990, Handel's marketing manager planned only one major change in the sales program: to increase the credit period to 60 days. All other marketing costs were expected to remain unchanged. Assuming that all customers choose to use the full 60 days to pay invoices, the sales manager has predicted an increase in sales to $270 million.

1. What are the current average outstanding accounts receivable? Current credit costs? Dollar variable contribution?

2. What are the comparable figures for the proposed 60-day plan?

3. How much more contribution do the new sales bring in? How much higher are costs of credit under the new credit plan? Would you recommend they proceed with the new plan?

4. How does your answer to Question 3 change if the following situations occur? (Try each of these separately.)
    a. the sales manager revises his sales forecast downward.
    b. your variable costs are forecasted to increase slightly as of next year (i.e., current variable costs not affected).

5. Recalculate the problem by hand, treating credit costs as additional variable costs. To maintain current variable dollar contribution, how much would total sales (in dollars) have to be under the new credit plan?

Exhibit 1. Handel Credit Policy Worksheet

Annual sales (in 000s)	$240,000<<	
Credit period	30<<	days
Cost of carrying accounts	20%<<	
Variable costs	40%<<	of sales

MACRO COMMANDS PROVIDED:
(Alt)C: To change estimates as indicated in Exhibit 1.
(Alt)P: To print screen.

Note: This problem is based on the Handel, Inc. case in Guiltinan and Paul's second edition manual.

File Name: COLBERT

8.2 COLBERT COMPANY

The Colbert Company is a manufacturer of lawnmowers, saws, electric drills, and a number of other tools and products for use around the house. Most of their output is sold to department stores, discounters, and hardware chains, who sell the products under the Colbert name or under their own name.

Colbert sells a line of power saws to one hundred small hardware chains across the country. The typical chain orders 500 saws a year, in monthly orders of about 40 to 45 saws per month. The saws are sold to the chains for $100 each, and Colbert's variable costs amount to $80 per unit. Colbert's order costs (which include sales contact and processing costs) average $400 per order per chain.

Colbert is thinking of offering a quantity discount to encourage the chains to place larger orders. For example, Colbert could offer a price discount to chains that purchase three months' supply of saws per order instead of only one month's supply. Thus, only four orders (rather than twelve) would have to be processed per year. Carrying extra inventory, of course, increases the chain's inventory costs, so not all chains will be receptive to this kind of deal. Based on experience with other hand tool sales, Colbert management knows that there is a relationship between the size of the price deal and the number of chains that will take advantage of the quantity discount. If the discount off regular price is $1.00, about 10% of chains will take advantage of the discount. If the discount is $3.00, about 30% of chains will buy on discount. (The total number ordered per year, 500, does not change, only the pattern of how many are bought per order and order frequency.) The accompanying computer program can be used to analyze the effects of price discounts of any level.

1. Try a few different price discounts. For each, what is the total reduction in total contribution margin due to the price discount? What is the total savings in order cost to Colbert?

2. What price discount provides the best net profit impact?

3. Is your answer to Question 2 sensitive to increases in variable cost or order cost?

4. (Set variable cost and order cost back to original levels.) Suppose the discount you suggest in Question 2 convinces the chains who take the discount price to order six times a year instead of four (no other changes to spreadsheet). How is the net profit impact affected? Why does it increase/decrease?

5. What assumptions are you making when you do this analysis?

6. What other benefits in addition to those included in the spreadsheet might be obtained by Colbert?

Exhibit 1. Colbert Company Price Discounting Policies

```
Quantity discount:              $0<<    per unit
                                Customers buying at:
                                Reg. Price      Disc. Price
                                ==========      ===========
Price                              $100            $100 per unit
Variable Cost                       $80<<           $80 per unit
Unit Var. Contr. Mgn.               $20             $20 per unit
Sales Volume                        500             500 units
Dollar Contr. Mgn.              $10,000         $10,000
Order Cost                         $400<<          $400 per order
Number of Orders/Year               12                4<<
Total Order Cost                 $4,800          $1,600
Reduction in Margin:                                 $0
Savings in order cost:                           $3,200
Total net profit impact:                             $0
Number of customers:                100               0
Net profit impact per
  customer:                                      $3,200
```

MACRO COMMANDS PROVIDED:
(Alt)C: To change estimates as indicated in Exhibit 1.
(Alt)P: To print screen.

File Name: LITEBAR

8.3 LITEBAR, INC.

Litebar, Inc. is a maker of portable bars sold to consumers through three kinds of retail outlets: specialty furniture stores, discount stores, and department stores. The company sells direct to each kind of retailer; company sales representatives are responsible for sales and for setting up retail displays.

The spreadsheet in Exhibit 1 provides complete information on sales, costs, and the basis for cost allocation across retail outlet type. The only costs included in the spreadsheet are those that are directly traceable to individual sales segments: shipping, sales, credit and order/billing costs. For example, costs of advertising are left out, even though Litebar spent $214,500 on advertising last year and is planning to spend the same amount again this coming year. The rationale is that Litebar would probably not reduce its advertising budget by eliminating one of the retail outlet types. As a rule of thumb, managers should attempt to assign only those costs that are influenced by the process of selling to each segment.

Exhibit 1. Litebar Inc. Contribution Analysis

	Spec. Furn. Stores	Discount Stores	Department Stores	Basis for Allocation
Sales	$300,000<<	$1,800,000<<	$1,200,000<<	Sales receipts
- Var. Costs:				
Labor	39,000	234,000	156,000	13% of sales
Materials	78,000	468,000	312,000	26% of sales
Var. Contrib.	183,000	1,098,000	732,000	
- Traceable Fixed Costs:				
Shipping	89,200<<	153,700	92,600	Delivery recs.
Sales	67,600<<	81,800	42,600	Sales reports
Credit	13,600<<	11,000	3,600	Bad-debt rep.
Orders/bill.	7,800<<	6,600	5,100	Charge/order
Contrib. to Nontraceable Ind. Cost and Profit	$4,800	$844,900	$588,100	

1. How would you compare the contributions made to profit by each of the retail outlet types? What opportunities are there for profit improvement? How do you know?

2. What would happen to total contribution to indirect costs and profit if the company implemented each of the following policies? (Try each policy separately and reset to original values before going on to the next.)
    a. Close down sales to specialty furniture stores.
    b. Eliminate credit to specialty furniture stores, which is forecasted to cut sales and order costs to these outlets by 15%.
    c. Shift sales-force emphasis away from specialty stores, which would reduce sales and order costs to specialty stores by 10% but would increase sales and order costs to each of the other store types by 5%.
    d. Require small-volume accounts to pay for their own shipping. It is anticipated that specialty store sales and order costs would decrease by 10% and shipping costs to specialty stores would decrease by 5% if this is done (no effects on sales to discounters or department stores).

3. What would you recommend that the firm do? You can recommend a course of action different from the four given above; if you do, make sure your assumptions regarding effect on sales, costs, and so on are reasonable.

MACRO COMMAND PROVIDED:
(Alt)P: To print screen.

Note: This problem was based on the PB Inc. example in Guiltinan and Paul's first edition, Chapter 12.

File Name: EASTERLY

8.4 EASTERLY FLOOR COVERINGS

Easterly produced a limited line of rugs and other floor coverings and sold the products through carpet wholesalers to 5000 department stores, furniture stores and carpet specialty stores. Wholesalers received a margin of 15% of the price paid by retailers and, in turn, performed selling, local warehousing, and credit functions for Easterly.

In the early 1970s, company officials began to rethink the sales and distribution policy. Easterly's market share had declined slightly, while those competing firms that sold directly to retailers seemed to be increasing their market shares.

By 1976, Easterly's sales to retailers had reached $50 million. Of this amount, 15% went to wholesalers, and an additional 25% went for other variable costs. However, half of the retail outlets carrying the Easterly line generated 90% of all sales.

Wholesalers generally called on each account about once per month on the average. In order to sell direct, Easterly would have to add substantially to its four-person sales force (which currently called only on wholesalers). The sales manager estimated that salespeople would cost about $40,000 per year in salary plus expense, with each salesperson capable of making 4.8 calls per day. (There were about 250 selling days per year.)

About one-half of each salesperson's time with a retailer was spent arranging displays and checking inventory. However, while retailers carried substantial amounts of inventory, their inventories reflected only a fraction of the styles, weaves, and colors available. Consequently, to provide rapid service to retailers in order to fill most orders, Easterly would have to rent warehouse space in about twenty locations at a cost of about $1,200,000 yearly and would have to carry the regional warehouse inventory burden formerly carried by wholesalers. Easterly's inventory-carrying cost was 25% of the average inventory (valued at the price paid by the retailer). Inventory turnover for the company was estimated at five times per year.

Finally, Easterly would have to provide retailers with trade credit. Normally, carpet retailers sought 60-day terms and the annual carrying cost of accounts receivable was estimated to be 20%.

1. There are three distribution policies to compare: Policy 1, sell through wholesalers; Policy 2, sell direct to 5000 accounts; Policy 3, sell direct to 2500 best accounts. For each of these, calculate the following:

a. Sales revenue to retail
b. Wholesale margin
c. Sales force costs
d. Warehouse costs
e. Inventory costs
f. Accounts receivable costs
g. Other variable costs
h. Contribution

A worksheet for calculating accounts receivable costs is provided as part of the accompanying computer package (see Exhibit 1). You should be able to calculate the rest of these values by hand.

2. What are the cost and profit implications of selling direct versus through retailers? Which policy would you recommend if you were considering only profit implications?

3. Suppose Easterly offered credit terms of 90 days. How would that change the contributions found in Question 1? Would this change your recommendation in Question 2?

4. Which type of channel will be most effective in building sales? Should Easterly drop the lower performing retail stores and concentrate on the top 50%? Consider other aspects to the problem besides the profit implications already discussed.

Exhibit 1. Easterly Floor Coverings Contribution Analysis and Accounts Receivable Worksheet

```
Sales to retailers:                    $50,000,000<<
Less:
  Wholesale margin:                     $7,500,000<<
  Sales force costs:                      $160,000<<
  Warehouse costs:                             $0<<
  Inventory costs:                             $0<<
  Accounts receivable costs:                   $0<<
  Other variable costs:                $12,500,000<<
Contribution:                          $29,840,000
```

WORKSHEET FOR ACCOUNTS RECEIVABLE COSTS

```
Sales to retail =                      $50,000,000<<
Credit period =                                60<<    days
Annual carrying cost =                         20<<    percent
```

Accounts receivable costs =
  sales to retail x (credit period/360 days) x carrying costs

MACRO COMMAND PROVIDED: (Alt)P: To print screen.

Note: This problem is based on the Easterly Floor Coverings case in Guiltinan and Paul's second edition manual.

File Name: SFCALL

8.5 SALES FORCE CALL PLANNING EXERCISE

Your company sells its products through a sales force that calls on industrial customers in the northeast. You are the company's sales force manager, and you are planning a schedule for one sales representative's activities over the next year.

Because of traveling times and distances, you have divided the sales rep's geographic region into three territories. Territory 1 has a sales potential of $70,000 per year; Territory 2 has a potential of $60,000; and Territory 3, $50,000. (See sales and cost information in Exhibit 1.) You have to decide how the sales rep should allot his time and effort across the three territories next year.

One would expect that the more effort (in terms of number of calls) made in a territory, the more sales would occur. At least, this should hold up to a point, as eventually a saturation level of effort would be reached, and sales would be maximized. Based on historical sales records and input from the sales rep, you have developed a set of estimates linking the number of visits made in each territory to expected sales levels. For example, in Territory 1, where the rep made 20 calls, current annual sales are at $40,000. You estimate that, if no calls were made in this territory, $5,000 of sales would still be made next year (due to repeat ordering). If the current call rate was boosted by 50% (from 20 to 30 calls), you project a sales level of $50,000 (This is called the plus-50 sales estimate.) The maximum sales rate in this territory with a saturation level of effort is estimated at $55,000. The same kind of estimates are made for each of the other two territories (see Exhibit 1).

Given these estimates, and expected variable and fixed costs, it is possible to find the optimal level of calls in each territory and to determine what level of sales and contribution to indirect costs and profit would be attained by this allocation of effort (see Exhibit 2).

This procedure is based on the first part of Lodish's (1971) CALLPLAN procedure for finding optimal sales plans. The full CALLPLAN model is much more elaborate and considers such factors as travel time and costs and time spent per call. This problem is similar to the "calibration phase" of CALLPLAN, in which the relationship between number of calls and sales level is specified. For more details, see information provided in the accompanying spreadsheet.

1. Suppose you need not worry about the sales rep's time or cost constraints: he can make as many calls as required in each territory. How many calls should he make in each territory to maximize total contribution to indirect costs and profit? What would be the corresponding sales level (in dollars)?

2. Now you must consider time as a constraint. Because of time spent with the customer on each sales call, and travel time between territories, the rep can make no more than 48 calls next year. What allocation of these 48 calls across the three territories provides the highest total contribution to indirect costs and profit? What is the corresponding sales level?

3. New competitive intelligence reveals that a major competitor will be pouring huge resources into this region in order to increase market share. You believe this will reduce the sales rep's effectiveness. Revise your maximum, minimum, and plus-50 estimates for each territory downward by 10%, and redo Questions 1 and 2 with the new estimates. Is the maximum total contribution to indirect costs and profit generated by this sales rep greatly affected?

Exhibit 1. Sales Estimates by Territory

	Terr. 1	Terr. 2	Terr. 3	Total
Current call rate	20	10	18	48
Sales potential	$70,000	$60,000	$50,000	
Current sales	$40,000	$28,000	$32,000	$100,000
Expected sales with no calls	$5,000<<	$8,000<<	$3,000<<	
Expected sales if calls incr. 50%	$50,000<<	$35,000<<	$37,000<<	
Expected sales with call saturation	$55,000<<	$40,000<<	$42,000<<	
Expected var. cost per call	$400	$600	$500	
Dir. fixed cost				$50,000

Exhibit 2. Contribution Analysis by Territory

	Terr. 1	Terr. 2	Terr. 3	Total
No. of Calls	20<<	10<<	18<<	48
Estimated Sales	$40,000	$28,000	$32,000	$100,000
Est. Var. Costs	$8,000	$6,000	$9,000	$23,000
Est. V.C.M.	$32,000	$22,000	$23,000	$77,000
Dir. fixed cost				$50,000
C.I.C.P.				$27,000

MACRO COMMAND PROVIDED: (Alt)P: To print contribution analysis.

PART 9: THE MARKETING PLAN

    9.1 Nor-East Dairies (NOREAST)
    9.2 Goodwell Company (GOODWELL)
    9.3 Elliott Corporation (ELLIOTT)
    9.4 Harpswell, Inc. (HARPSWEL)
    9.5 Worldwide Food Products, Inc. (WORLD)

File Name: NOREAST

9.1 NOR-EAST DAIRIES

Nor-East markets a line of dairy products in a three-state area. In 1980, the company began introducing specialty snack cheeses, all of which were well received by retail supermarkets and consumers. Because some of the products had seasonal appeals and because dairy section shelf space was limited, retailers tended to stock some of Nor-East's cheese products only for a few months at a time. However, 82% of all supermarkets in the region stocked at least some Nor-East cheese products all the time.

In 1983, the company developed a new "beer cheese," a somewhat spicy cheese in which beer was a minor ingredient. Taste tests indicated that consumers would be very receptive to the product, and by December 1983, Jim O'Brien, Nor-East's director of marketing, was developing a 1984 marketing plan for the product. In light of the company's prior success, O'Brien was certain that all supermarkets that regularly stocked Nor-East cheeses would stock the beer cheese for at least the first two months of 1984. Because the sales volume was highly uncertain, O'Brien decided to develop only a six-month marketing plan at the present time. If it became clear that the beer cheese line would at least break even for the first six months (i.e., have at least a zero total contribution), then O'Brien would develop the rest of the annual plan.

O'Brien's initial marketing plan called for a $150,000 advertising budget for January and February to stimulate awareness of the product. Additionally, retailers would be given free merchandise allowances during February if they agreed to feature Nor-East beer cheese in their local newspaper advertising during the last two weeks of that month. Although the cost of these allowances would depend on the number of retailers subscribing to the program, O'Brien's best estimate was that 30% of the retailers would subscribe at a cost to Nor-East of $30,000. Nor-East's variable contribution on manufacturer's sales was approximately 40%.

Additionally, top management had assigned a monthly charge of $10,000 as the beer cheese product's share of selling expenses. Other direct fixed costs for the beer cheese line were expected to average $15,000 per month.

1. How many sales does Nor-East need over the six months to break even? (Calculate by hand.)

2. Prepare a six-month plan for Nor-East beer cheese. Clearly state objectives, strategies, programs, and budgets. Assume that

the plan will show a total contribution of zero for the six-month period, and develop what you consider to be a reasonable distribution of dollar sales over the six months. Enter your sales projections into the spreadsheet by replacing zeros as shown in Exhibit 1.

3. What specific performance measures should O'Brien select for controlling the plan? At what intervals should actual and planned performance be compared for the various measures you select?

4. It is now the end of March. Each month's sales have been 15% lower than forecasted. You are still determined to break even by the end of June, and you believe that spending an additional $50,000 in advertising during both April and May to stimulate consumer demand is necessary.
    a. Now how much sales revenue do you need to sell between April 1 and June 30 to break even?
    b. Develop a revised sales plan for April through June, with a realistic distribution of sales figures across the months. Enter your revised sales figures in place of the zeros in Exhibit 2.

Exhibit 1. Nor-East Dairies Original Marketing Plan (all entries in $000s)

	Jan.	Feb.	Mar.	Apr.	May	June	Total
Sales	0<<	0<<	0<<	0<<	0<<	0<<	0
PVCM	0.4	0.4	0.4	0.4	0.4	0.4	0.4
VCM	0	0	0	0	0	0	0
DFC:							
Adv.	75	75	0	0	0	0	150
S.Pro.	0	30	0	0	0	0	30
Sales	10	10	10	10	10	10	60
Other	15	15	15	15	15	15	90
Total DFC	100	130	25	25	25	25	330
Tot.Cont.	-100	-130	-25	-25	-25	-25	-330

Exhibit 2. Nor-East Dairies Revised Marketing Plan (all entries in $000s)

	Jan.	Feb.	Mar.	Apr.	May	June	Total
Sales	0	0	0	0<<	0<<	0<<	0
PVCM	0.4	0.4	0.4	0.4	0.4	0.4	0.4
VCM	0	0	0	0	0	0	0
DFC:							
Adv.	75	75	0	50	50	0	250
S.Pro.	0	30	0	0	0	0	30
Sales	10	10	10	10	10	10	60
Other	15	15	15	15	15	15	90
Total DFC	100	130	25	75	75	25	430
Tot.Cont.	-100	-130	-25	-75	-75	-25	-430

MACRO COMMANDS PROVIDED:
(Alt)G: To save PrintGraph file of your sales projections.
(Alt)P and (Alt)Q: To print the original and revised plans.

Note: This problem is based on the Nor-East Dairies case in Guiltinan and Paul's second edition, Chapter 14.

File Name: GOODWELL

9.2 GOODWELL COMPANY

Goodwell was a moderately-sized firm that produced a variety of prescription drugs and nonprescription products. The company used its own sales force to sell all its products to large chain drug stores and used wholesalers to reach grocery stores (which stocked some of its nonprescription products).

In 1983, the company had developed an athlete's foot spray and was contemplating introducing it to the market. Product testing had revealed that the product was just as effective as Goodwell's athlete's foot powders and ointments. Goodwell's existing products held about a 10% share of this market. Industry sales were forecast to be $60 million for 1984 and to grow by $2 million per year through 1989.

Company policy dictated that all new products should earn or generate enough cash flow (before taxes) discounted at 25% to recover the initial cash investment within four years. Goodwell had already invested $250,000 in research and development on this product and knew that an additional investment of $750,000 would be needed for equipment (to be depreciated over five years).

Test market results suggested that the new product would obtain a market share of about 4%, with one-half of the projected sales coming from Goodwell customers. Advertising expenditures to introduce the spray would be $400,000 in 1984. But after that, all three forms would be advertised jointly at the current rate for joint powder/ointment advertising: $600,000 per year. No other marketing expenses would be incurred, but annual fixed production costs for the new product would be $100,000 direct and $100,000 for the product's share of indirect expenses. Based on anticipated material and labor costs, Goodwell expected a variable contribution margin on retail sales of 50% (the same as on ointment and powder).

1. Based on this information, should Goodwell proceed with the new product? Show calculations.

2. How low could the market share be for the company to just pay back the equipment investment in four years?

3. Would your recommendation in Question 1 change if any of the following contingencies occurred? (Try each separately, resetting to original values before continuing.)
    a. The resulting market share was only 3%.
    b. The spray was charged with one-third of the advertising budget for 1986-1987.
    c. The market growth rate was zero.

Exhibit 1. Goodwell Cash Flow Analysis (all entries in 000s)

	1984	1985	1986	1987
	====	====	====	====
Industry growth per year	0<<			
Industry sales	$0<<	$0	$0	$0
Company share	0.00%<<			
Company sales	0	0	0	0
Incremental sales	0	0	0	0
Var. Contrib. Mgn.	0<<			
Variable Contrib.	0	0	0	0
- Increm. Direct				
Advertising	0<<	0<<	0<<	0<<
Production	0<<	0<<	0<<	0<<
Depreciation	0<<	0<<	0<<	0<<
Increm. Profit	0	0	0	0
+ Depreciation	0	0	0	0
Increm. Cash Flow	0	0	0	0
Discount Rate	0.00%<<			
Disc. Cash Flow	0	0	0	0
Cumul. Cash Flow	0	0	0	0

MACRO COMMAND PROVIDED: (Alt)P: To print screen.

Note: This problem is based on the Goodwell case in Guiltinan and Paul's first edition manual.

File Name: ELLIOTT

9.3 ELLIOTT CORPORATION

The Elliott Corporation is a large manufacturer of electronic products. It is among the market share leaders in many high-tech product categories; is well known for its research and development laboratories, which have an enviable success record; and is generally thought of as manufacturing high-quality products. Corporate management was examining the projected five-year sales and profit figures for a newly developed product and was evaluating the product's feasibility.

The evaluation system used by Elliott consists of three benchmarks: return on capital (ROC), return on sales (ROS) and residual profit. The company sets a target return on capital (which currently is 10%) and determines the level of profit necessary to achieve this target return. Any profit over and above this level is considered residual profit. In evaluating a new product such as this one, management projects residual profit levels for each of the first five years of production, and also determines the net present worth of annual residual profits.

In projecting sales and profits for the new product over the next five years, Elliott management made use of the following information and estimates:

    a. First year sales are projected at $3,700,000, with a projected annual growth rate of 10% over the first five years.
    b. Variable costs of sales amount to 54% of sales.
    c. The allotments to research and development are projected as follows (figures in thousands of dollars):

	Year 1	Year 2	Year 3	Year 4	Year 5
Research	94	150.1	230.1	336	470
Development	312	324.5	337.5	351	365

    d. Merchandising costs for this class of product typically run at 15-18% of sales: management estimates these costs at 15.58% of sales for this product.
    e. General and administrative expenses amount to 2.6% of variable costs of sales.
    f. The tax rate is 50%.
    g. Inventory is maintained at about 12-15% of sales; management is estimating average inventory at 14.15% of sales.
    h. The plant where the product will be manufactured is valued at $1,500,000; an additional investment of $50,000 toward the plant will be made each year.
    i. Other capital is estimated at 10% of sales.

1. Evaluate the new product's finances using ROS, ROC, and residual profit analysis.

2. At what sales levels does the present value of the firm's residual profits just equal zero? How do these sales levels compare to projected sales levels?

3. Test the sensitivity of ROS, ROC, and present worth of residual profit with respect to the following changes. (Try each separately and reset to original level before continuing.)
    a. changes in first-year sales level, assuming projected growth rate is achieved,
    b. changes in projected sales growth rates (try 7% and 13%),
    c. increases in variable costs of sales as a percentage of sales revenue,
    d. increase in the cost of capital to 12%.

4. Do the finances for this product look promising? What other factors might you consider in deciding whether to begin full-scale production and marketing of this product?

Exhibit 1. Elliott Corporation Residual Profit Analysis (all dollar figures in $000s)

	Year 1	Year 2	Year 3	Year 4	Year 5
Sales	3700.00<<	4070.00	4477.00	4924.70	5417.17
Cost of sales	1998.00	2197.80	2417.58	2659.34	2925.27
Gross revenue	1702.00	1872.20	2059.42	2265.36	2491.90
Research	94.00	150.10	230.10	336.00	470.00
Development	312.00	324.50	337.50	351.00	365.00
Merch.	576.42	634.06	697.46	767.21	843.93
Gen. + Adm.	51.95	57.14	62.86	69.14	76.06
Tot. Expenses	1034.36	1165.80	1327.92	1523.35	1754.99
Pretax Profit	667.64	706.40	731.50	742.01	736.91
Taxes	333.82	353.20	365.75	371.00	368.45
Net Profit	333.82	353.20	365.75	371.00	368.45
Avg. Invent.	522.98	575.27	632.80	696.08	765.69
Avg. Net Plant	1500.00	1550.00	1600.00	1650.00	1700.00
Avg. Oth. Cap.	370.00	407.00	447.70	492.47	541.72
Avg. Tot. Cap.	2392.98	2532.27	2680.50	2838.55	3007.41
% ROC	13.95	13.95	13.64	13.07	12.25
% ROS	9.02	8.68	8.17	7.53	6.80
Cost of Cap.	10.00<<	10.00	10.00	10.00	10.00
Profit Reqd.	239.30	253.23	268.05	283.86	300.74
Resid. Profit	94.52	99.97	97.70	87.15	67.71

Present Worth of Annual
Residual Profit: $343.52
Estimates: Annual growth rate in dollar sales: 10.00%<<
           Percent variable cost of sales: 54.00%<<

MACRO COMMANDS PROVIDED:
(Alt)C: To change estimates as shown in Exhibit 1.
(Alt)P: To print residual profit analysis.

<u>Note</u>: This case was developed with the assistance of Prof. Roger J. Calantone of the University of Kentucky.

File Name: HARPSWEL

9.4 HARPSWELL, INC.

A product manager for Harpswell, Inc., a small manufacturer of office equipment, is preparing the 1987 marketing plan for one of the firm's products, the 5000X machine.

In 1986, this product held a 10% market share of a fast-growing market for a multipurpose laminating and reproducing machine. The 1986 profitability statement for the product is given in Exhibit 1. (The company sells directly to buyers, using its own sales force so no distributor margins are involved.)

Top management wants to increase the market share for this product by acquiring new customers. The company believes that its product has special features that will allow each customer to meet its own specific needs. However, the features are complex, and a technical sales force is required to communicate the product's benefits. Harpswell uses advertising to increase awareness among potential buyers of the Harpswell name as the manufacturer of this machine. At the present time, the market is believed to be only moderately price-sensitive, because performance risks are as great as economic risks. Accordingly, a parity pricing approach will be employed.

By examining industry sales data and the allocation of competitive selling efforts, Harpswell has learned that the rate of purchase of this product has been low in certain buying industries, especially in the northeast. Consequently, a target market for the coming year has been chosen on the basis of industry type (for purposes of media selection) and region (for purposes of sales-force allocation).

On the basis of discussions with top management, the product manager has established two objectives for 1987:

1. attaining a 14% market share
2. achieving a target contribution of $1 million.

For 1987, industry sales are expected to grow to 200,000 units and variable costs are expected to increase to $125 per unit.

Exhibit 1. 1986 Profitability Statement for the 5000X

Unit sales	18000	
Selling price	$250	
Variable Cost per Unit	$120	
Sales Revenue		$4,500,000
Variable Cost		$2,160,000
Variable Contribution Margin		$2,340,000
Controllable Direct Costs:		
Advertising	$300,000	
Sales and Distribution	$1,200,000	
Total		$1,500,000
Total contr. to ind. costs and profit		$840,000

1. With the market share and target contribution objectives as given, answer the following:
   a. What is the required sales target in units?
   b. How much required sales revenue does this sales target translate into?
   c. What would be the resulting variable contribution margin?
   d. How much of this contribution would be left over to cover marketing expenses (advertising and sales)?
   e. Given that last year's marketing budget was $1,500,000, how high an increase in marketing budget could the company afford for this product?

2. Suppose that, based on his understanding of the marketplace, the product manager feels that the company could sell 20,000 units unconditionally (without additional support from advertising or sales force). He also believes that the new marketing program will result in additional sales of 7600 units. He therefore projects the overall sales of the 5000X in 1987 to be 27,600 units. With this in mind, determine the following:
   a. whether the company will meet its market share objective.
   b. whether the company will meet its total contribution objective.

3. What could the firm do to meet its objectives? Should the objectives be revised downward? What options are available to Harpswell now?

4. How great would the response to the proposed marketing program have to be for the company to meet its market share objective?

5. Redo Questions 1, 2, and 4 for a market share target of 13% and a profit objective of $800,000. Assume that the marketing budget you recommend will yield sales (over and above the unconditional sales level) of 6400 units.

Exhibit 2. Sales Forecasts and Profitability Analysis for 1987

Industry sales forecast (units):	200000
Unconditional sales forecast:	20000
Market share objective:	0%<<
Sales target:	0
Profit objective (target total contribution):	$0 <<
Price per unit:	$0.00 <<
Variable costs per unit:	$0.00 <<

BUDGET FOR 1987 ANNUAL PLAN

Projected sales in units:	
Unconditional forecast	20000
+ Sales from addl. adv. & sales efforts	0
Total	20000
This represents a market share of	10%

MACRO COMMANDS PROVIDED:
(Alt)P and (Alt)Q: To print first and second spreadsheets.
(Alt)C: To make changes to spreadsheet as indicated in Exhibit 2.

Note: This problem is based on the Harpswell, Inc. example in Quiltinan and Paul's first edition, Chapter 13.

File Name: WORLD

9.5 WORLDWIDE FOOD PRODUCTS, INC.

Worldwide Food Products manufactures several different consumer product lines. One of the most profitable is a thirst-quenching energy drink, especially popular during the active summer months. You have been called in to develop a business plan for this product for the upcoming year.

Competition is fierce in this industry. The Worldwide brand currently holds 19% of the market for this kind of drink. Since you know that market shares and sales in this industry are very responsive to changes in advertising outlay, you decide to use an ADBUDG approach to project next year's sales by season. Brand sales have also traditionally been sensitive to Worldwide's price relative to the industry average, so the model you have developed adjusts its projected market shares accordingly. Based on interviews with Worldwide senior management, you have obtained the following market share and advertising cost projections (Exhibit 1):

a. seasonal advertising budget required to maintain current market share of 19%: $50,000

b. minimum share projected if advertising were cut to zero: 4%

c. maximum share projected with saturation advertising: 23%

d. share projected with a 50% increase in advertising budget: 21%

e. variable cost per unit: $2.17

f. current Worldwide price to dealers: $2.79 per unit

g. average competitor's price to dealers: $2.79 per unit

You believe that these share estimates do not vary by season; however, total industry sales does in fact fluctuate. Your best projections for industry sales for the next four seasons are: winter, 4 million units; spring, 5 million; summer, 6 million; fall, 3.5 million.

1. At a price of $2.79 and an advertising budget of $50,000 per season, what is the projected total contribution to indirect costs and profits generated by this product? Holding price constant, can you improve on this contribution by increasing advertising? What seasonal advertising budget maximizes total contribution? (See Exhibit 2.)

2. Worldwide would like to experiment with a higher selling price to boost per-unit margins. Increase selling price to dealers to $2.99, and leave seasonal advertising budget at the contribution maximizing level you found in Question 1. To what extent is total contribution affected by the price move? Can you improve upon this contribution by varying advertising?

3. (Reset price to $2.79 and advertising to the contribution maximizing level of Question 1.) How sensitive is the total contribution to changes in each of the following? (Try each separately, resetting to original value before continuing.)
    a. a 10% increase in variable cost per unit.
    b. a 10% increase in average competitive price per unit.

4. (Reset all estimates to original values.) You have reason to believe the ADBUDG estimates as originally provided were overstated. Scale down the minimum, maximum, and plus-50 share estimates by one percentage point each, and redo Question 1.

Exhibit 1. Worldwide Food Products ADBUDG Analysis

Current share	19%
Maintenance Budget ($000)	$50
Minimum share	4%<<
Maximum share	23%<<
Plus-50 share	21%<<
Variable costs per unit	$2.17<<
Ave. compet. price	$2.79<<

Exhibit 2. Worldwide Food Products Business Plan

Price:			$2.79<<	
Advertising per Season:			$50,000<<	

	Winter	Spring	Summer	Fall
Ind.Sales (000)	4000	5000	6000	3500
Co. Share	19%	19%	19%	19%
Co. Volume (000s)	760.00	950.00	1140.00	665.00
Co.Sales Rev.($000)	2120.40	2650.50	3180.60	1855.35
Contr.Mgn. ($000)	471.20	589.00	706.80	412.30
- Fixed Costs($000)				
Advertising	50.00	50.00	50.00	50.00
Other Fixed	100.00	100.00	100.00	100.00
Total Fixed Costs	150.00	150.00	150.00	150.00
Total Contr.($000)	321.20	439.00	556.80	262.30

Sales Rev. for Year ($000)	9806.85
Total Contr. for Year ($000)	1579.30

MACRO COMMANDS PROVIDED:
(Alt)A: To change ADBUDG estimates.
(Alt)O: To change variable cost per unit and average competitive price.
(Alt)C: To change selling price and seasonal advertising level.
(Alt)P: To print screen.

REFERENCES

Agostini, M.M. 1961. How to Estimate Unduplicated Audiences. *Journal of Advertising Research*, 1(3), March: 11-14.

Bass, Frank M. 1969. A New Product Growth Model for Consumer Durables. *Management Science*, 15, January: 215-227.

Little, John D.C. 1970. Models and Managers: The Concept of a Decision Calculus. *Management Science*, 16(4), April: B466-B485.

Lodish, Leonard M. 1971. CALLPLAN: An Interactive Salesman's Call Planning System. *Management Science*, 18(4), Part II, December: 25-40.

Parfitt, J.H. and Collins, B.J.K. 1968. Use of Consumer Panels for Brand Share Prediction. *Journal of Marketing Research*, 5, May: 131-146.

Rao, Ambar G. and Lilien, Gary L. 1972. A System of Promotional Models. *Management Science*, 19(2), October: 152-160.

Silk, Alvin J. and Urban, Glen L. 1978. Pre-Test Market Evaluation of New Packaged Goods: A Model and Measurement Methodology. *Journal of Marketing Research*, 15, May: 171-191.

Urban, Glen L. 1975. PERCEPTOR: A Model for Product Positioning. *Management Science*, 21(8), April: 858-871.

Urban, Glen L. and Hauser, John R. 1980. *Design and Marketing of New Products*. Englewood Cliffs, N.J.: Prentice-Hall.

Vidale, H.L. and Wolfe, H.B. 1957. An Operations Research Study of Sales Response to Advertising. *Operational Research Quarterly*, 5: 370-381.